MOVE IT!
STUDENTS' BOOK

CAROLYN BARRACLOUGH, KATHERINE STANNETT

SERIES CONSULTANT: CARA NORRIS-RAMIREZ

Starter Unit

Vocabulary

• Countries and nationalities

1 Match the countries (1–8) to the nationalities (a–h).

Country	Nationality
1 Spain	a Greek
2 England	b Mexican
3 Brazil	c French
4 France	d Portuguese
5 Italy	e English
6 Portugal	f Spanish
7 Mexico	g Brazilian
8 Greece	h Italian

2 Match the countries from Exercise 1 to the letters (a–h) on the map. Do you know any other countries?

a *England*

• Numbers

3 Add/Subtract the numbers. Write the answer.

1 fifteen + twenty-six *forty-one*
2 one hundred twelve – nineteen
3 eighty-five + seventy-nine
4 one thousand six – eleven
5 sixty-one + six hundred two

```
  15
+ 26
----
  41
```

4 Listen. Write the numbers you hear in your notebook.
1.2

• Spelling

5 Say the letters to spell these words.
1.3 Listen and check.

1 B-R-A-Z-I-L-I-A-N
2 E-L-E-V-E-N
3 B-A-C-K-P-A-C-K
4 M-P-3 P-L-A-Y-E-R
5 S-E-C-O-N-D-A-R-Y

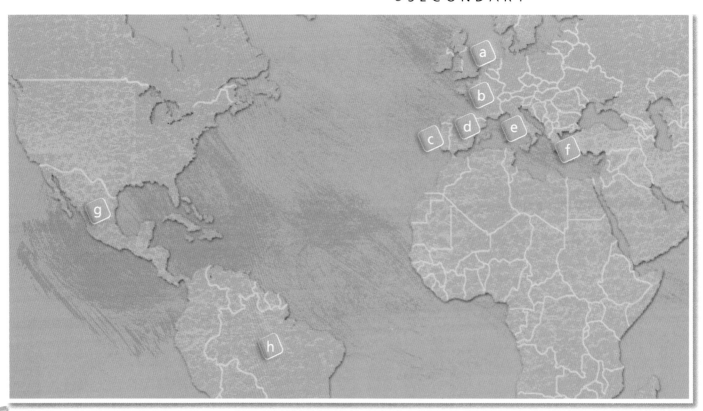

• Classroom objects

6 **Look for one minute. Remember and write the objects in your notebook.**

1 *interactive whiteboard*

• Days of the week and months of the year

7 **Put the days in the correct order. Which day is your favorite?**

- Wednesday
- Saturday
- Friday
- Sunday
- Monday *1*
- Tuesday
- Thursday

8 **Find four months in each line.**

1 cow*november*armarchapplejanuarybreaddecember
2 daycookjuneolyaprilgremondayoctoberpenciljuly
3 februarygreenmayaugustairportcarseptember

• Classroom language

9 **Match the sentences to the speaker.**
1.4 **Is it a student (S) or a teacher (T)? Listen and repeat.**

1 Open your books! *T*
2 Can you repeat … , please?
3 How do you spell … ?
4 Listen carefully.
5 I'm sorry, I don't understand.
6 Please be quiet!
7 Check your answers.
8 How do you say … in English?
9 What's the homework?

Grammar • To be

1. Study the grammar table.

Affirmative	Negative
I'm (am)	I'm not
You're (are)	You aren't (are not)
He's (is)	He isn't (is not)
She's (is)	She isn't (is not)
It's (is)	It isn't (is not)
We're (are)	We aren't (are not)
They're (are)	They aren't (are not)
Questions and short answers	
Am I … ?	Yes, I am. / No, I'm not.
Is he/she/it … ?	Yes, he/she/it is. No, he/she/it isn't.
Are you/we/they … ?	Yes, you/we/they are. No, you/we/they aren't.

Watch Out!
Subject pronouns
- I
- You
- He
- She
- It
- We
- They

2. Choose the correct options.

1 My friend Leo *is* / *are* American.
2 We *aren't* / *isn't* from London. We are Spanish.
3 I *are* / *am* in a new class.
4 *Is* / *Are* they at the park?
5 You *is* / *are* in the classroom!

3. Complete the sentences.

1 He *is* a boy but she …. a boy; she …. a girl!
2 …. he a doctor?
3 I …. French, I'm Italian. I come from Milan.
4 …. you twelve years old? You are very tall!
5 …. it a cat? No, I think it's a dog.
6 You …. in English class with Ms. Taylor.

• *Wh* questions

4. Study the grammar table.

Wh questions
What's your name?
Where are you from?
How old are you?
When is your birthday?
Why are you happy?
Who is your sister?

5. Complete the questions.

1 *Where* is Paris?
 It's in France. Paris is the capital of France.
2 …. is your brother?
 He's fifteen. And my little sister is two.
3 …. is that?
 It's a bicycle.
4 …. are you happy?
 I am happy because it's my birthday today.
5 …. is your best friend?
 My best friend is Pedro.
6 …. is Halloween?
 It's in October.

6. Make questions.

1 name / What's / your ?
 What's your name?
2 you / from / Where / are ?
3 How / are / you / old ?
4 is / your / birthday / When ?
5 you / happy / Why / are ?
6 Who / best friend / your / is ?

7. In pairs, ask and answer the questions in Exercise 6.

• This/That/These/Those

8 **Study the grammar table.**

Singular		Plural	
This is a pen.	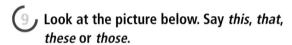	These are erasers.	
That is a desk.		Those are chairs.	

9 **Look at the picture below. Say *this, that, these* or *those*.**

1 *That* is an interactive whiteboard.
2 .... are backpacks.
3 .... are chairs.
4 .... are pens.
5 .... is a pencil.
6 .... are erasers.
7 .... are rulers.
8 .... is a calculator.

> **Watch Out!**
> This is a pen. NOT ~~This is pen.~~
> These are chairs. NOT ~~These are a chairs.~~

Reading

1 Look at the text. How many people are in the Wildlife Club?

Welcome to ...
The Wildlife Club!

- The Wildlife Club ... **what** is it?
  It's a great nature club at our school.
- The Wildlife Club ... **when** is it?
  It's on Thursday afternoons, from 3:30 to 4:30.
- The Wildlife Club ... **who** is in it?
  Say hello to our Wildlife Club members!

I'm Nick. I'm in 8th grade, and I'm 13 years old. My favorite animal is my dog, Sunny. The Wildlife Club is cool! Wildlife and nature are very important to me.

I'm Julia, and this is my brother, Leo. I'm 12, and Leo is 8. He is in the Wildlife Club because animals and nature are his favorite things.

2 Read the text again. Are the statements true (T) or false (F)?

1.5

1 The Wildlife Club is an arts club. *F*
2 The Wildlife Club is on Friday afternoons.
3 Nick is 13 years old.
4 Sunny is a rabbit.
5 Leo and Julia are friends.

Listening and Speaking

3 Look at the photo. Find the new member of the Wildlife Club.

4 Listen to the conversation. Who is the new member?
1.6

5 Listen to the conversation again and complete the form.
1.6

Wildlife Club
New Member Form

Name   *Monica*

Age   ....

Grade   ....

What's your favorite animal?

....

6 Listen to the conversation again. Are these statements true (T) or false (F)?
1.6

1 Monica is in 7th grade.
2 Nick is in 7th grade.
3 Sunny is in the Wildlife Club.

7 In pairs, ask and answer to complete your profile.

Wildlife Club
New Member Form

Name   ....

Age   ....

Grade   ....

What's your favorite animal?

....

✓ **My assessment profile:** page 127

1 My World

Vocabulary • Objects

1 Match the photos to these words. Then listen, check and repeat.

1.7

> camera
> cell phone
> comics *1*
> DVD
> game console
> guitar
> ice skates
> laptop
> magazine
> MP3 player
> poster
> skateboard
> wallet
> watch

2 Match the definitions to seven objects from Exercise 1.

1 It's a musical instrument. *guitar*
2 It's a movie.
3 It's a computer.
4 It's a small clock.
5 They're stories with superheroes.
6 It's a board with wheels.
7 It's a big picture.

3 Listen and find the missing letter.

1.8
1 wallet /   3 camera
2 comics   4 skateboard

4 Think of three words with missing letters. In pairs, ask and answer.

What letter is missing?
W - A - C - H.

It's T.

Good.

Brain Trainer Activity 3
Go to page 58

Reading

1 Look at the photos. Who has these things: Lisa (L) or Emilio (E)?

1 a skateboard
2 a camera
3 comics
4 posters

2 Read and check your answers to Exercise 1.

3 Read the text. How many objects do Lisa and Emilio mention?
1.9

4 Read the text again. Answer the questions.
1.9
1 Where is Lisa from? *She's from Canada.*
2 Where is Emilio from?
3 What is Lisa a fan of?
4 What is Emilio a fan of?
5 Name *The Simpsons* objects.
6 Name the soccer objects.

5 What about you? In pairs, ask and answer.
1 What TV show/team/sport are you a fan of?
2 Who is your favorite TV character/athlete?

I'm a fan of *Glee.*

I'm a New York Yankees fan.

Fans of the Month

Simpsons fan!

My brother and I are *Simpsons* fans. We have about two hundred comics, and they have very funny stories and pictures. Do you have a *Simpsons* comic?

The Simpsons computer game is cool, but we don't have a *Simpsons* DVD. I have a *Simpsons* watch and a big skateboard with Bart Simpson on it. My brother doesn't have a skateboard, but he has a guitar with a picture of Homer on it. It's awesome!

Oh, and guess what? My name is Lisa ... but my brother's name isn't Bart!

Lisa, Canada

Soccer fan!

I'm from Mar del Plata in Argentina. We have a great soccer team here. I have a soccer shirt, a scarf, a wallet and a backpack ... and a lot of posters on my bedroom walls! Mom and Dad are big soccer fans, too. Dad has a blue laptop, a blue cell phone and a blue car!

I also have photos of some players on my camera. Messi is my favorite player. He is an excellent goal scorer!

Emilio, Argentina

Grammar • Have

Affirmative		
I/You/We/They	have	a new DVD.
He/She/It	has	

Negative		
I/You/We/They	don't have (do not have)	a new DVD.
He/She/It	doesn't have (does not have)	

Questions		
Do I/you/we/they	have	a new DVD?
Does he/she/it	have	

Short answers
Yes, I/you/we/they do. / No, I/you/we/they don't.
Yes, he/she/it does. / No, he/she/it doesn't.

Grammar reference page 108

Watch Out!
do not → don't
does not → doesn't

1 Study the grammar table. Complete the rules.

1 We say I / .... / .... / .... have or don't have.
2 We say he / .... / .... has or doesn't have.
3 The question form of they have is .... ?
4 The short form of do not have is .... .
5 The short form of does not have is .... .

2 Choose the correct options.

1 Carla and Luisa has / have posters of Lady Gaga.
2 Elena doesn't have / don't have a Twilight DVD.
3 Do / Does your parents have a laptop?
4 I has / have a camera in my backpack.
5 Harry doesn't have / don't have a Superman comic.
6 Do / Does Angela have a new watch?

3 Find the subject + verb. Write the full form in your notebook.

1 He doesn't have a new game console.
   He does not have
2 They don't have a laptop.
3 We don't have posters for the classroom.
4 The teacher doesn't have an MP3 player.

4 Complete the text with *have* or *has*.

My dad is a DJ. He ¹*has* a radio show. He gets famous people on his show. He ².... a lot of autographs from the famous people. He ³.... autographs from Will Smith and Angelina Jolie. But he doesn't ⁴.... an autograph from a sports player. My favorite singer is Katy Perry, but I don't ⁵.... her autograph. Do you ⁶.... an autograph from a famous person?

Pronunciation Short forms

5a Look at the verbs. Find the short forms
1.10 and listen.

1 I don't have a cell phone.
2 She doesn't have a magazine.
3 They don't have my ice skates.

b Listen again and repeat.
1.10

6 What about you? In pairs, ask and answer about these objects.

DVD	guitar	magazine
MP3 player	skateboard	watch

Do you have an MP3 player?

Yes, I do.

Vocabulary • Adjectives

1 Match the adjectives (1–7) to the opposite adjectives (a–g).
1.11 **Then listen, check and repeat.**

1 bad
2 cheap
3 difficult
4 popular
5 boring
6 new
7 small

a expensive
b unpopular
c interesting
d good
e big
f easy
g old

Word list page 43   **Workbook** page 116

2 **Choose the correct options. Then listen, check and repeat.**
1.12

1 Help! I have this game.
It's really *easy* / *difficult*.

2 We have a sports game for
your console. It's from 2007,
so it's *new* / *old*.

3 I have two Rihanna posters.
She's great—she's very
popular / *unpopular*.

4 Look at this camera. It's $750,
so it's *cheap* / *expensive*.

5 I have about fifteen
schoolbooks! I have a
big / *small* backpack.

6 I have these cool DVDs.
They're very *good* / *bad*.

7 Do you have *New Moon*?
It's an *interesting* / *boring*
novel. Read it now!

3 Listen and guess the adjective.
1.13 **More than one answer may
be possible.**

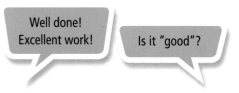

Well done!
Excellent work!

Is it "good"?

4 Complete the sentences with
adjectives from Exercise 1.

1 The movie *The Pirates of
the Caribbean* is *good*.
2 A Ferrari is .... .
3 Keira Knightley is .... .
4 The Harry Potter books
are .... .
5 Brazil is .... .
6 I think English is .... .
7 Usher's songs are .... .

5 Choose one thing from each
group. Use an adjective and
write a sentence in your
notebook.

• computer game / book /
movie / song
• sports star / actor / singer
• object in your school / home

The computer game is difficult.

6 Look at the objects in Exercise 2.
In pairs, ask and answer.

Is the camera
expensive?

Yes, it is.

Brain Trainer
Activity 4
Go to page 58

Chatroom Talking about position

Speaking and Listening

1 **Look at the photo and answer the questions.**

   1 Who is in Nick's room?
   2 Name three objects in Nick's room.

2 **Listen and read the conversation.**
1.14 **Answer the questions.**

   1 Is Nick's room big or small? *It's small.*
   2 Does Nick have a game console?
   3 Does Nick have a soccer game?
   4 Are Nick's ice skates on the bed?
   5 What is under the desk?

3 **Act out the conversation in groups of three.**

Julia	This is a nice room!
Nick	Thanks. It's small, but it's OK.
Julia	Oh look, Sunny's in your room.
Nick	Sit, Sunny. Good dog.
Leo	Is this your game console, Nick?
Nick	Yes, it is.
Leo	Cool! What games do you have?
Nick	I have a new soccer game—it's really difficult!
Leo	Where is it?
Nick	It's next to the game console.
	Oh, my ice skates are on the desk! Sorry.
Leo	Hey, Nick, what's that under the desk?
Nick	Oh, it's my skateboard.
Leo	Great. I have one, too.

Say it in your language ...

Cool!

Great.

4 **Look back at the conversation. Who says what?**

1 It's next to the game console. *Nick*
2 Sunny's in your room.
3 What's that under the desk?
4 My ice skates are on the desk!

5 **Read the phrases for talking about position.**

Talking about position
Sunny's in your room.
Where is it?
It's next to the game console.
My ice skates are on the desk!
What's that under the desk?

6 **Match the pictures to these words.**

behind   in   in front of   next to   on   under

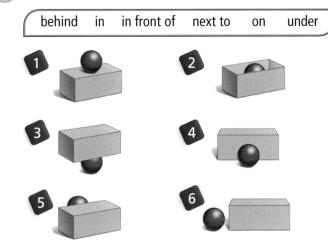

7 **Listen to the conversation. Act out**
1.15 **the conversation in pairs.**

Ryan Where's the ¹ magazine?
Tania Is it ² on the desk?
Ryan No.
Tania Look. It's ³ under the desk.

8 **Work in pairs. Replace the words in purple in Exercise 7. Use these words and/or your own ideas. Act out the conversation.**

> Where's the laptop?

> Is it next to the desk?

1 DVD / game console / cell phone
2 behind / next to / under
3 in front of / on

Grammar • Possessive adjectives and Possessive *'s*

Possessive adjectives		Possessive *'s*
I	my	**One person**
you	your	Monica's bag.
he	his	Nick's dog.
she	her	
it	its	**Two or more people**
we	our	My parents' car.
they	their	John and Tom's room.

Grammar reference page 108

1 **Study the grammar table and learn.**

2 **Make sentences. Change the <u>underlined</u> words.**

1 It's <u>Julia's</u> watch.
It's her watch.
2 That's <u>my parents'</u> room.
3 Those are <u>my brother's and my</u> DVDs.
4 It's <u>Mr. Green's</u> laptop.
5 Are these <u>Anna's</u> books?
6 This is <u>the boy's</u> ball.

3 **Copy the sentences. Put the apostrophe in the correct place.**

1 I have my moms wallet.
I have my mom's wallet.
2 Do you have Andys cell phone?
3 Here is my grandparents house.
4 This is the teachers MP3 player.
5 Where is Marinas dads camera?
6 My sisters names are Olivia and Lina.

4 **What about you? In pairs, ask and answer questions about five objects in the classroom.**

> Is this your pen?

> No, it's Rafa's pen.

Reading

1 Look quickly at the text and the photos. Answer the questions.

1 What type of text is it?
  a a quiz
  b a competition
  c an interview
2 Who are the characters in the photo?
  a They're from a movie.
  b They're from a book.
  c They're from a play.

My dad's collection.

My dad in his *Star Wars* costume.

Help!

Dad Has an Embarrassing Hobby!

This week's problem page interview is with Nicole from Montreal, Canada.

■ **Do you have a special collection, Nicole?**

No, I don't have a collection, but my dad has a *Star Wars* collection. It's his favorite movie, but it's an old movie now, and I'm not a big *Star Wars* fan. Here's a photo of Dad with his friends at a *Star Wars* convention. Just look at their costumes—it's really embarrassing!

■ **Is it a big collection?**

Yes, it is. Dad has hundreds of props and costumes from the *Star Wars* movies. He has DVDs and posters in the living room. He has Luke Skywalker's *lightsaber* in the dining room, and *Star Wars* books and magazines in his bedroom, too. I have a *Star Wars* bed in my room with Darth Vader on it. Yuck! Our house is full!

■ **Is this a problem?**

Well, it's OK because we have a big shed in the backyard, but guess what? That's full of *Star Wars* things, too. Dad is happy with his collection, but Mom isn't happy because *Star Wars* things are very expensive.

Key Words		
embarrassing	convention	costumes
props	shed	

2 Read and check your answers to Exercise 1.

3 Read the interview again. Are the statements
1.16 true (T) or false (F)?

1 Nicole is a fan of *Star Wars* movies. *F*
2 Nicole's dad has a *Stars Wars* costume.
3 Her dad has thousands of *Star Wars* things.
4 Nicole has a *Star Wars* bed.
5 Her parents have a small shed in the backyard.
6 *Star Wars* things aren't cheap.

Listening

1 Listen to three interviews. Match the speaker
1.17 to the interview.

Interview 1   a Peter's mom
Interview 2   b Peter's brother
Interview 3   c Peter

2 Listen again. Answer the questions.
1.17

1 Who has a *Karate Kid* collection?
  a Peter's brother   b Peter's mom   c Peter
2 What is Peter's mom's opinion?
  a The collection is big.
  b The collection is small.
  c The collection is cheap.
3 What is Peter's brother's opinion of *The Karate Kid*?
  a It's cool.   b It's great.   c It's boring.

Writing • A personal profile

1 Read the Writing File.

> **Writing File** Punctuation 1
>
> **We use punctuation to make our writing clear.**
>
> - **We use capital letters (A, B, C …) for the names of people, places, songs, games and groups.**
> - **We also use capital letters for the first person I.**
> - **We use periods (.) at the end of sentences.**
> - **Apostrophes (') can show missing letters—for example, in short forms.**
> - **Apostrophes can also show possession.**

2 Read the profile. Match the words in blue to the rules in the Writing File.

My favorite things

My name's ¹Billy, and ²I'm eleven years old. I'm from ³Chicago. It's a big city in ⁴Illinois. My favorite thing is my new game console. I ⁵don't have a lot of games because ⁶they're expensive. I have about five. My favorite is ⁷*Guitar Hero* because I have an electric guitar for this game. ⁸It's a great game, and the ⁹game's songs are good. My favorite song is ¹⁰*Ruby* by ¹¹Kaiser Chiefs.

3 Rewrite the sentences. Use capital letters, periods and apostrophes.

1 his names luke *His name's Luke.*
2 shes my sister
3 im thirteen years old
4 our teachers name is john day
5 they dont have a game console

4 Read the profile again. Answer the questions.

1 How old is Billy? *He's eleven years old.*
2 Where is he from?
3 What are his two favorite things?
4 Why doesn't he have a lot of games?
5 Why is *Guitar Hero* his favorite game?
6 What is his favorite song?

5 Answer the questions.

1 What's your name, and how old are you?
2 Where are you from?
3 What are your favorite things?
4 Give extra information about your favorite things.

6 Write a description of you and your favorite things. Use "My favorite things" and your answers from Exercise 5.

> **My favorite things**
>
> **Paragraph 1**
> - Your personal information
>   *My name is … , and I'm … .* (age)
>   *I'm from … .*
>
> **Paragraph 2**
> - Your favorite things
>   *My favorite thing is … / My favorite things are … and … .*
> - Extra information
>   *I have … .* (number)
>   *I don't have … .*
>   *My favorite … is … because … .*

> **Remember!**
> - Use capital letters, apostrophes and periods in the correct places.
> - Use the vocabulary in this unit.
> - Check your grammar and spelling.

Refresh Your Memory!

Grammar • Review

1 Make affirmative and negative sentences with *have*.

	Felipe	Adriana and Damon
1 a guitar	✓	✗
2 a skateboard	✗	✓
3 a game console	✗	✗
4 an MP3 player	✓	✓

1 *Felipe has a guitar.*

2 Make questions and short answers about the things in Exercise 1.

1 *Does Felipe have a guitar? Yes, he does.*

3 Complete the sentences with the correct possessive adjective.

1 I have *my* lunch in this bag.
2 Do you have .... MP3 player?
3 Mr. Smith has .... watch.
4 Mrs. Jones doesn't have .... laptop.
5 We have .... magazines.
6 They have .... cameras.

4 Rewrite the sentences. Use possessive *'s* or *s'*.

1 Kayla / laptop / is new
   Kayla's laptop is new.
2 My brother / camera / is expensive
3 Jessica and Oscar / dog / is small
4 My teacher / book / is interesting
5 Fabio / favorite soccer player / is Ronaldo
6 My cousins / DVD / is old

Vocabulary • Review

5 Complete the sentences with these words.

cell phone	comics	laptops
MP3 player	skateboard	watch

1 The teacher doesn't have any *comics* in her classroom.
2 My .... is in my bag.
3 I have some new songs on my .... .
4 I don't have a .... , but I have a bike.
5 What time is it? I don't have my .... .
6 The school has .... for students.

6 Find seven adjectives.

from   **small**   the   get   **unpopular**
fan   name   **easy**   **cheap**   **look**
expensive   **room**   **bad**   **boring**

Speaking • Review

7 Look at the picture and complete the conversation.
1.18 Then listen and check.

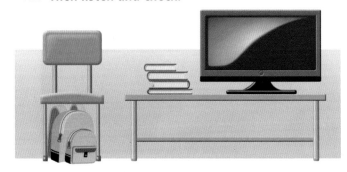

A Where's my backpack?
B It's there, ¹ .... the chair.
A Are my schoolbooks ² .... my bag?
B No, they aren't.
A Where are they?
B They're ³ .... the table, ⁴ .... the TV—here!

Dictation

8 Listen and write in your notebook.
1.19

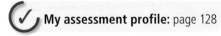
✓ My assessment profile: page 128

20th-Century Painting

On this page are examples of two different styles of early-20th-century painting: Cubism and Pointillism. One painting is a still life—a painting of objects such as vases, bowls or mugs. The other painting is a landscape—this is a painting of the countryside.

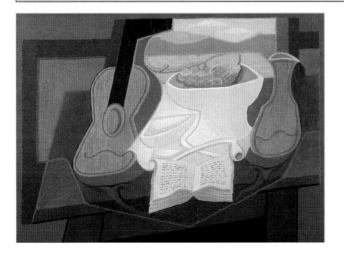

Guitar and Fruit Bowl

This picture has a guitar, a fruit bowl, a bottle and a book in it. Juan Gris's style of painting is Cubism. The picture has a lot of geometrical shapes, and the colors are not very bright. This is typical of Cubist paintings. Other famous Cubist artists are Pablo Picasso and Georges Braque.

Washing in the Sun

This painting is from 1905. There is a basket with some laundry in it. The trees are blue, and there are long shadows. Pellizza da Volpedo's style of painting is called Pointillism. Pointillist paintings have very small dots of color. Georges Seurat and Paul Signac are other famous Pointillist artists.

Reading

1 Match the artists to the pictures.

1 Pellizza da Volpedo
2 Juan Gris

2 Read about the two paintings.
1.20 **Answer the questions.**

1 Which two styles of painting can you see on this page?
2 Name three Cubist artists.
3 Which of these paintings is a landscape? Which is a still life?
4 Which style of painting uses bright colors?

My Art File

3 In pairs, find out about another famous 20th-century painting. Think about:

- the artist
- the style of painting
- other artists in the same style
- the objects/people in the painting
- why you like it

4 Design a poster about your painting. Use your notes from Exercise 3 to help you. Then present your poster to your class.

② Around Town

Vocabulary • Places in a town

1 Match the places in the picture to these words. Then listen, check and repeat.

1.21

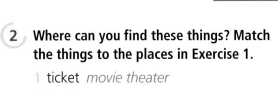

- bank
- bus station
- café
- hospital *1*
- library
- movie theater
- museum
- park
- police station
- post office
- shopping mall
- sports complex
- town square
- train station

Grammar
There is/There are;
Some/Any, Can/Can't
for ability

Vocabulary
■ Places in a town;
■ Action verbs

■ **Speaking**
Orders and warnings

Writing
A description of a town

Word list page 43
Workbook page 117

2 Where can you find these things? Match the things to the places in Exercise 1.

1 ticket *movie theater*
2 book
3 ball
4 tree
5 money
6 coffee

3 Read the clues and find the places in the picture.

1 It's behind the shopping mall.
   train station
2 It's behind the park.
3 It's next to the post office.
4 It's in front of the movie theater.
5 It's next to the shopping mall.
6 It's in front of the police station.

4 In pairs, make a list of other places in a town.

supermarket, playground

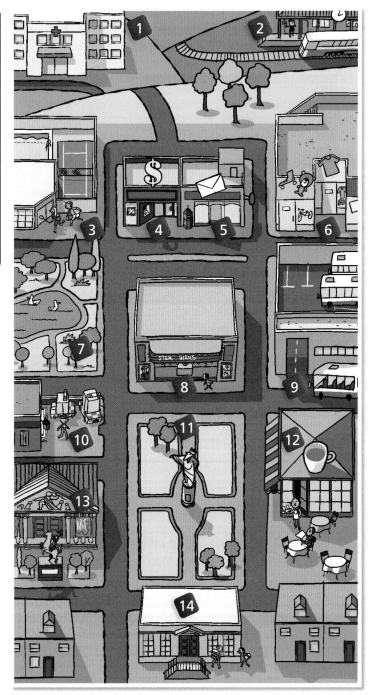

**Brain Trainer
Activity 3**
Go to page 59

Reading

1 Look at the text. What do you think it is about?

a parks
b virtual towns
c shopping malls

2 Read the text and check your answer to Exercise 1.

3 Read the text again. Are the statements true (T) or false (F)?
1.22

1 TanyaCity doesn't have any museums. *F*
2 TanyaCity has a library.
3 Fabville doesn't have any houses.
4 Fabville has a school.
5 Garboton has some stores.
6 Garboton has a train station.

4 What about you? Invent your Cybertown. In pairs, ask and answer.

1 What's the name of the town?
2 Where is it?
3 What places does it have? Where are they?

What's the name of the town?

It's MusicTown.

Cybertown
It's Our Town, It's Your Town

Tanya

My Cybertown is TanyaCity. I have a big house and a lot of friends. There are two shopping malls next to my house, with a lot of great stores. There's a museum and a park in front of the library, and there are some big houses behind my school. TanyaCity is a beautiful town.

Ben

My Cybertown is Fabville. It's really cool. I ♥ sports, and Fabville has a sports complex and three parks. My house is next to a big library. In the town square, there is a bank and a small post office, and there's a very big hospital. Next to the hospital there's a great café. In Fabville there aren't any schools!

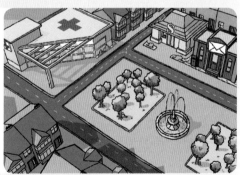

Sanjay

Garboton is my Cybertown. It has very good connections—there's a train station and a bus station. There's a town square in Garboton, and there are some stores, but there isn't a shopping mall. There isn't a museum or a library, but there's a big police station. It's my police station! I'm the Chief of Police in Garboton!

Grammar • There is/There are; Some/Any

Affirmative
There's (There is) a museum.
There are some houses/two shopping malls.

Negative
There isn't (is not) a library.
There aren't (are not) any schools.

Questions and short answers	
Is there a hospital?	Yes, there is. No, there isn't.
Are there any houses?	Yes, there are. No, there aren't.

Grammar reference page 110

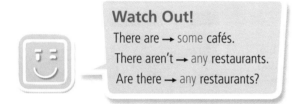

Watch Out!

There are → some cafés.
There aren't → any restaurants.
Are there → any restaurants?

1 Study the grammar table. Complete the rules with *there is, there are, there isn't* and *there aren't*.

1 We use .... and .... with singular nouns,
   e.g., *a museum, a cat, a house.*
2 We use .... and .... with plural nouns,
   e.g., *some/any stores, a lot of schools.*

2 Choose *There is* or *There are* to complete the sentences.

1 *There is* a big shopping mall in our town.
2 .... three Canadian girls in my school.
3 .... some books under your bed.
4 .... a big party on Saturday. It's my birthday!
5 .... a new interactive whiteboard in my classroom.
6 .... two swimming pools in this sports complex.

3 Complete the conversation. Then listen and check.

1.23
Tom What's in your town, Emma?
Emma ¹ *There's* a big movie theater and an international school. ² .... any parks. ³ .... any parks in your town?
Tom Yes, ⁴ .... . ⁵ .... some beautiful parks, and ⁶ .... a shopping mall called GoShop. ⁷ .... a sports complex in your town?
Emma No, ⁸ .... . But ⁹ .... a modern art museum.

4 Make questions and answers.

1 any good movies / on TV? (✗)
   Are there any good movies on TV?
   No, there aren't.
2 a cell phone / in your bag? (✓)
3 a swimming pool / in your house? (✗)
4 any American students / in your class? (✓)
5 any libraries / in your town? (✗)

5 Look at the information about Sandra's backpack. Find and correct five mistakes in the text.

There isn't a wallet.

My backpack	
pen	✓
wallet	✗
DVDs	✗
apple	✗
MP3 player	✗
laptop	✓
books	✗
magazine	✓

There's a pen in my backpack, and there's a wallet. There are some DVDs, and there's an apple and an MP3 player. There isn't a laptop. There aren't any books in my backpack, but there's a magazine.

6 What about you? Imagine you have a new backpack. What do you have in it? Write six sentences.

In my backpack, there's ... .

Vocabulary • Action verbs

1 Match the pictures to these words. Then listen,
1.24 check and repeat.

bike	climb *1*	dance	fly	juggle	jump
play	run	sing	skate	swim	walk

Word list page 43   **Workbook** page 117

2 Match the verbs (1–8) to the phrases (a–h).

1 play *d*
2 swim
3 juggle
4 climb
5 jump
6 bike
7 sing
8 run

a six balls
b a song
c a tree, a mountain
d a game, soccer, the guitar
e to school
f 100 meters, in the pool
g very high
h a marathon

3 Make complete sentences with the information in Exercise 2.

1 *I play soccer.*

Pronunciation
Silent letters

4a Listen and find
1.25 the silent letter in each word.

1 walk
2 climb
3 guitar
4 talk
5 know

b Listen again and
1.25 repeat.

Brain Trainer
Activity 4
Go to page 59

Chatroom Orders and warnings

Speaking and Listening

1 Look at the photo. Are these things in the photo?

1 backpack ✓	5 dog	8 laptop
2 book	6 food	9 map
3 canoes	7 ice skates	10 wallet
4 cell phone		

2 Listen and read the conversation.
1.26 Are the statements true (T) or false (F)?

1 There is a lake in the park. *T*
2 The park isn't a good place for a picnic.
3 Monica has the map.
4 The food is in Nick's bag.
5 Leo is very careful.
6 Julia isn't very happy.
7 At the end, their lunch is in the lake.

3 Act out the conversation in groups of four.

Monica	Where are we now? Look at the map, Nick.
Nick	OK, we're at the lake. The park's a really good place for our picnic.
Leo	A picnic! Great! Oh, and our lunch is in my backpack. Apples! Watch me! I can juggle!
Julia	Leo, be careful!
Monica	Leo! Don't play with our food!
Nick	Come on, everyone. Let's go!
Leo	Hang on, guys. Wait for us!
Julia	Don't shout, Leo!
Leo	OK. Look! I can dance in the canoe.
Julia	Leo! Please, don't do that. Stop!
Leo	Oh no! Help!
Monica	Are you OK, Leo? Can you swim?
Leo	Yes, I can, but there's a small problem.
Nick	What?
Leo	Our lunch is in the lake.
M, N & J	Oh Leo!

Say it in your language …
Let's go!
Hang on.

4 Look back at the conversation. Complete the instructions.

1 W <u>a</u> <u>t</u> <u>c</u> <u>h</u> me!
2 B_ careful!
3 Don't p _ _ _ with our food!
4 W _ _ _ for us!
5 Don't s _ _ _ _!
6 S_ _ p!

5 Read the phrases for giving orders and warnings.

Orders
Watch me!
Don't play … !
Wait for us!
Don't shout!
Please, don't do that.

Warnings
Be careful!
Stop!
Help!

6 Listen to the conversations. Act out
1.27 the conversations in pairs.

Julia   Leo, don't play with ¹ our food.
Leo   OK, Julia. But don't shout!

Julia   Leo, don't ² swim in the lake.
Leo   OK, Julia. But don't shout!

7 Work in pairs. Replace the words in purple in Exercise 6 with these words. Act out the conversations.

Leo, don't play with my camera.

OK, Julia. But don't shout!

1 my cell phone / my laptop / my book

2 run / climb trees / dance in the canoe

8 Act out the conversations again with your own words and ideas.

Grammar • *Can/Can't* for ability

Affirmative
I/You/He/She/It/We/They can juggle.

Negative
I/You/He/She/It/We/They can't dance.

Questions and short answers
Can I/you/he/she/it/we/they play the guitar?
Yes, I/you/he/she/it/we/they can.
No, I/you/he/she/it/we/they can't.

Grammar reference page 110

1 Study the grammar table. Choose the correct rule, *1* or *2*.

1 We say *can/can't* + *to* + verb.
2 We say *can/can't* + verb.

2 Look at the table. Then read the sentences and say *Jon*, *Dan* or *Matt*.

	sing	dance	juggle
Jon	✓	✗	✗
Dan	✗	✗	✓
Matt	✓	✓	✗
Anna	✗	✓	✓
Meg	✓	✓	✗

1 This boy can sing, and he can dance, but he can't juggle. *Matt*
2 This boy can't dance, and he can't juggle, but he can sing.
3 This boy can juggle, but he can't sing, and he can't dance.

3 Complete the sentences for Anna and Meg.
Anna can … .
Meg can … .

4 Make questions with *can*.

1 ride a bike? *Can you ride a bike?*
2 juggle?
3 sing?
4 play tennis?
5 play the piano?
6 climb trees?

Reading 🔉

1 Look at the photos. What animals can you see?

Great Parks in New York City

▶ **Central Park**
This is a very big park in the middle of Manhattan in New York City—it's 3.4 square kilometers. You can walk around the park and look at the trees, plants and lakes. You can watch the beautiful ducks in the lakes. You can also see a lot of fountains in this park. There are over 40 fountains here! You can bring your bike and ride around the park. There is an amazing view of the park from Belvedere Castle. You can play baseball or have a picnic in the park, or you can go fishing in the lake. You can also get lunch at one of the many food carts in the park. The food is great!

▶ **Bronx Park**
This famous New York park is the home of the Bronx Zoo and the New York Botanical Garden. You can walk for three kilometers along the Bronx River. There are many species of fish and birds to see here. It's a great experience! You can visit the Bronx Zoo in the southern half of the park to see animals from other parts of the world—for example, flamingos. The park also has playgrounds, basketball courts, and football and soccer fields.

Key Words

| view (n) | castle | to play baseball |
| to go fishing | species | experience |

2 Read the text and check your answer to Exercise 1.

3 Read the text. Answer the questions.

1.28
1 Where is Central Park?
 It is in the middle of Manhattan in New York.
2 What animals can you see in Central Park?
3 What famous building has an amazing view of Central Park?
4 What two places can you find in Bronx Park?
5 How long is the part of the Bronx River in Bronx Park?
6 What animals can you see near the river?

4 Read the text again. Choose *Central Park* (CP)
1.28 or *Bronx Park* (BP).

1 It's in the middle of New York City. *CP*
2 You can see flamingos here.
3 You can have a picnic here.
4 You can walk along a river.
5 You can play soccer.
6 You can ride a bike in this place.

Listening 🔉

1 Listen to the audition. Say *Latika, Kate,*
1.29 or *Latika and Kate.*

TALENT WANTED!

**Tuesday, November 7
Auditions at the Regal Movie Theater,
3 p.m.**

1 She can climb trees.
2 She can swim.
3 She can't sing.
4 She can dance.
5 She can jump up high.
6 She can run really fast.

Writing • A description of a town

1 Read the Writing File.

> **Writing File** Linking words
> - There's a movie theater and a library in my town.
> - There's a swimming pool, but there isn't a sports complex.
> - Jess can't dance, but she can sing.
> - I can't swim or ride a bike.
> - There isn't a shopping mall or a park.

2 Read Emma's description of her hometown. Find examples of *and*, *or* and *but*.

My Hometown

In my hometown, there is a swimming pool, (and) there's a library, but there isn't a sports complex or a museum. There are a lot of houses and stores, but there aren't any movie theaters. There are two restaurants, and there are four cafés. There are some parks, and there's a shopping mall, but there isn't a bus station or a train station. There is a post office, but there isn't a bank. my hometown is small, but it's great.

3 Choose the correct options.
1 I can play soccer, *and / but* I can't play tennis.
2 In Paris there are a lot of restaurants *and / but* cafés.
3 There isn't a police station *but / or* a bank.
4 There aren't any new students at my school, *and / but* there are two new teachers.
5 We can have a picnic *and / but* ride our bikes.

4 Read Emma's description again. What does she have in her hometown?
1 a swimming pool ✓
2 a library
3 a sports complex
4 a museum
5 some houses
6 some stores
7 some parks
8 a shopping mall
9 a bus station
10 a train station
11 a post office

5 Imagine a town or think about your hometown. What is in your town? Take notes. Use the list from Exercise 4.

6 Write a description of your town. Use "My town" and your notes from Exercise 5.

> **My town**
> 1 Name
>   *My town is called ... .*
> 2 Description
>   *In ... there is a/are some ... .*
>   *In ... there isn't a/aren't any ... .*
> 3 Conclusion
>   *My town is ... .*

> **Remember!**
> - Use *and*, *or* and *but*.
> - Use the vocabulary in this unit.
> - Check your grammar, spelling, and punctuation.

Refresh Your Memory!

Grammar • Review

1 **Choose the correct options.**

1 There *is / are* two parks behind my school.
2 There *is / are* a calculator on my desk.
3 There *isn't / aren't* a train station in my town, but there *is / are* a bus station.
4 There *isn't / aren't* any comics in my bag.
5 **A** *Is / Are* there a post office next to the shopping mall?
   B No, there *isn't / aren't*.
6 **A** *Is / Are* there any posters in your classroom?
   B Yes. There *is / are* five posters in our classroom.

2 **Look at the list. Make sentences.**

There is one Spanish student in Class 5b.

International School Class 5b	
Spanish students	1
Greek students	0
French students	5
English students	2
Brazilian students	1
Portuguese students	0
Mexican students	4

3 **Complete the text with *can* or *can't* and the verbs.**

My brother, James, ¹ *can climb* (✔ climb), and he
² .... (✔ juggle), but he ³ .... (✗ run) fast. My sister,
Hatty, ⁴ .... (✔ dance), but she ⁵ .... (✗ sing).
I ⁶ .... (✗ dance), and I ⁷ .... (✗ juggle),
but I ⁸ .... (✔ swim).

4 **Make questions and answers.**

1 you / speak English?   ✔
  Can you speak English? Yes, I can.
2 your friends / skate?   ✗
3 your teacher / swim?   ✗
4 Fred / play chess?   ✔
5 Fred's dog / dance?   ✗
6 your dad / fly a plane? ✗

Vocabulary • Review

5 **Look at the pictures and complete the places.**

1 *library*   2 t .... s ....   3 h ....   4 c ....

5 p ....   6 s .... c ....   7 p .... o ....   8 b .... s ....

6 **Complete the sentences with these verbs.**

bike	sing	juggle	run
~~jump~~	dance	climb	play

1 Trev can *jump* very high.
2 Dave and Sarah can .... beautiful songs.
3 I can't .... the guitar.
4 My dad can .... six balls.
5 I can't .... up that tree!
6 My sister can .... the tango.
7 I can't .... to school because I don't have a bicycle.
8 Can you .... fast?

Speaking • Review

7 **Complete the sentences with these words.**
1.30 **Then listen and check.**

Be	bike	jump	Open	shout	~~swim~~

1 Don't *swim* in the lake!
2 .... quiet!
3 .... your book.
4 Don't .... in the schoolyard.
5 Don't .... on the desks!
6 Don't .... in the library.

Dictation

8 **Listen and write in your notebook.**
1.31

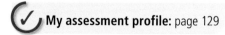
My assessment profile: page 129

Fazila Shirindel's Profile

Age
14 years old

Home country
Afghanistan

City
Kabul

Fazila and Skateistan

Fazila is a 14-year-old girl from Qalai Zaman Khan in Kabul, Afghanistan. Her family is very poor, and Fazila's life is difficult, but she is happy because she is a student at a school in Kabul. The school is called "Skateistan," and it's the first skateboarding school in Kabul.

Skateistan has a big indoor skate park and some classrooms with computers. Children can study English, computer science, journalism, art and music there. There's a special "Back to school" program for children who aren't in school. There are separate school days for boys and for girls because, in Afghanistan, girls and boys don't do activities together, and there are also special classes for disabled children.

After the classes, there is a 50-minute skateboarding lesson for all the girls in Fazila's class. Fazila doesn't have a skateboard, but she can borrow one from the school.

Now Fazila is very good at skateboarding, and she is also a teacher at Skateistan. "Life is hard for me because my family is poor," says Fazila. "But when I'm at Skateistan, I'm in a nice place."

Reading

1 **Read Fazila's profile. Answer the questions.**

1 How old is Fazila?
2 Where does she come from?

2 **Read about Fazila. Are the statements true (T) or false (F)?**
1.32

1 Fazila lives in Afghanistan. *T*
2 There aren't any classrooms in Skateistan.
3 Children can study English at Skateistan.
4 Boys and girls work together in schools in Afghanistan.
5 Fazila has a skateboard.
6 Fazila is happy at school.

Class discussion

● Can you skateboard?
● Do you think Skateistan is a good idea? Why?/Why not?
● Would you like a skateboarding school in your town?
● What special schools are there in your country?

3 School Days

Vocabulary • Daily routines

1 Match the pictures to these phrases. Then listen, check and repeat.

1.33

brush my teeth
clean up my room
do homework
get dressed
get up   *1*
go home
go to bed
have breakfast
have dinner
have lunch
meet friends
start school
take a shower
watch TV

2 Complete the sentences with phrases from Exercise 1.

1 I *get up* in the morning, and I *take* a shower.
2 I .... breakfast, then I .... my teeth.
3 I .... my friends on the bus.
4 I start .... at 9:00 a.m. My favorite class is math.
5 We .... lunch at 1:00 p.m.
6 I .... my homework after school. I study in my room.
7 In the evening, I .... TV with my family.
8 We .... to bed at 10:30 p.m. on school days.
9 I .... my room on Saturdays.

3 What words can follow these verbs?

1 brush *my teeth*   2 have   3 get   4 go

4 In pairs, make a statement about your day. Your partner guesses *true* or *false*.

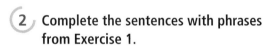

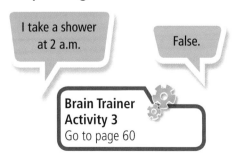

I take a shower at 2 a.m.

False.

Brain Trainer Activity 3
Go to page 60

Reading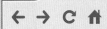

1 **Look at Maisie's family photo. Answer the questions.**

1 How many brothers does she have?
2 How many sisters does she have?
3 How many people are in her family?

2 **Read and check your answers to Exercise 1.**

3 **Read Maisie's blog again. Put these things**
1.34 **in the order Maisie does them.**

a play with brothers and sisters
b take a shower
c have breakfast *1*
d do homework
e go to school
f clean up the living room

4 **Read Maisie's blog again. Complete the sentences.**
1.34
1 Life in Maisie's house *is fun, but it's difficult, too.*
2 Maisie's family is .... .
3 Every morning, Maisie is in the bathroom for .... .
4 Maisie's parents don't have a car; they have .... .
5 Maisie has dinner at .... .
6 After 8 p.m., Maisie .... .

5 **What about you? In pairs, ask and answer.**

1 Do you have a big family?
2 How many brothers and sisters do you have?
3 Can you watch TV on school days?
4 Can you meet your friends after school?

> How many brothers and sisters do you have?

> I have two sisters.

A Day With ... My Big Family

My name is Maisie Hall, and I have five brothers and sisters! Life in our house is fun, but it's difficult, too.

On school days, I get up very early, at 6 a.m., but I don't take a shower right away. I have my breakfast first. Our family is big, so we don't have breakfast together. After breakfast I take a shower and get dressed. I only have five minutes in the bathroom before my sister knocks on the door!

At 8 a.m. we go to school in our minivan. It has ten seats, it's big, and it's fun!

School starts at 8:30 a.m., and we go home at 3 p.m. After school I don't watch TV. I clean up the living room for my mom, and I play with my brothers and sisters.

We have dinner all together at 6 p.m. My baby brother goes to bed at 7 p.m., and my other brothers and sisters go to bed at 8 p.m. Then I can work!

From 8 p.m. to 9 p.m. I do my homework, read a book or watch TV with my parents. After that I brush my teeth and go to bed.

Me and my family

Me

Grammar • Present simple: affirmative and negative

Affirmative		
I/You/We/They	get up	at 7 a.m.
He/She/It	gets up	
Negative		
I/You/We/They	don't (do not) get up	at 7 a.m.
He/She/It	doesn't (does not) get up	

Grammar reference page 112

Watch Out!

he / she / it → looks, watches, studies

1 Study the grammar table. Choose the correct options to complete the rules.

1 We add -s to the verb after *I, you, we, they / he, she, it.*
2 We use the words *don't* and *doesn't* to make the *affirmative / negative* of the Present simple.

Pronunciation -s endings

2a Listen to the -s endings.
1.35   likes → /s/   plays → /z/   watches → /ɪz/

b Listen and say /s/, /z/ or /ɪz/.
1.36
1 gets up	5 eats
2 has	6 dances
3 cleans	7 does
4 watches	8 goes

c Listen again and repeat.
1.36

3 Choose the correct options.

1 I *get / gets* up early and have breakfast.
2 My teachers *has / have* lunch at school.
3 They *has / have* dinner at 6 p.m.
4 We *goes / go* to the movies on Wednesdays.
5 Tom *meet / meets* his friends after school.
6 You *does / do* your homework before dinner.

4 Make negative sentences.

1 Josh has breakfast at 9 a.m.
Josh doesn't have breakfast at 9 a.m.
2 Adam goes to school by train.
3 I do Sudokus.
4 Lorenzo and Tina have lunch at one o'clock.
5 Anita plays tennis on Saturdays.
6 Ella goes to bed at 9:30 p.m.
7 We have dinner together.
8 You speak Chinese.

5 Complete the descriptions. Then guess the person.

get dressed	~~get up~~	get up	go
have	not have	not get up	

1 Every Saturday I ¹ *get up* at 7 a.m., and I ² ....
in my old clothes. First, I clean out the barn
on our farm, and then the animals ³ ....
breakfast. My parents and I ⁴ .... breakfast
early. We eat eggs and toast at about 10 a.m.

2 I ⁵ .... early on Saturday. I watch TV in bed, and
I ⁶ .... at 11 a.m. In the afternoon, my friends
and I ⁷ .... to the park and play soccer. My dog,
Sunny, likes soccer, too!

6 What about you? Write affirmative and negative sentences about your weekend.

I watch TV on Saturday.

Vocabulary • School subjects

1 Match the pictures to these words. Then listen, check and repeat.

1.37

art	computer science	English	French
geography	history	literature	math *1*
music	PE	science	social studies

Word list page 43
Workbook page 118

2 Jimmy can't find the right classroom. Listen and say the class.

1.38

1 Classroom 1 *math*
2 Classroom 2
3 Classroom 3
4 Classroom 4
5 Classroom 5
6 Classroom 6

3 Match these activities to subjects from Exercise 1.

1 write essays
   literature, history …
2 speak in pairs
3 use a computer
4 move your body
5 work with numbers
6 sing
7 read books
8 draw or paint
9 work with maps
10 do experiments
11 talk about society
12 write stories

4 What about you? In pairs, ask and answer.

1 What classes do you have on Monday?
2 Who is your art teacher?
3 What days are your English classes?
4 Are you good at math?
5 Do you have PE today?
6 What is your favorite class?

What classes do you have on Monday?

I have history, math, English and PE.

Brain Trainer
Activity 4
Go to page 60

Chatroom Time

Speaking and Listening

1 Look at the photo.

1 Where are Monica and Nick?
2 What objects can you see in the photo?

2 Listen and read the conversation. Match
1.39 the phrases to make sentences.

1 Monica meets Nick *b*
2 Monica gets up early
3 Monica lives
4 Nick has a
5 Nick's class starts

a on a farm.
b at a quarter past eight.
c at nine o'clock.
d because the bus leaves at seven fifteen.
e history class first.

3 Act out the conversation in pairs.

Monica	Hi, Nick! You're early.
Nick	Really? What time is it?
Monica	It's a quarter past eight.
Nick	Why are you early?
Monica	Because the bus from our town leaves at seven fifteen.
Nick	You're lucky to live on a farm. I love farms.
Monica	Yes, I know. Do you want to come over on Saturday?
Nick	Sure! Great idea! Thanks.
Monica	Great! What class do you have now?
Nick	I have history first.
Monica	What time does it start?
Nick	It starts at nine o'clock. What time is it?
Monica	It's eight twenty. See you later!

Say it in your language …
I know.
See you later!

4 Look back at the conversation. Find the times Nick and Monica talk about.

1 *a quarter past eight ...*

5 Read the phrases for asking and answering about time.

Asking about time	Answering about time
What time is it? What time does it start? What time does it finish?	It's a quarter past eight. It's eight twenty. At seven fifteen. It starts at nine o'clock. It ends at half past one.

6 What time is it?

1 7:15 *It's a quarter past seven. / It's seven fifteen.*
2 11:25
3 8:05
4 2:50
5 3:30

7 Listen to the conversation. Act out the conversation in pairs.
1.40

Girl What time is it?
Boy It's [1] a quarter past eleven.
Girl What time is our [2] French class?
Boy It starts at [3] eleven twenty. We're early.
Girl What time does it end?
Boy It ends at [4] twelve ten.

8 Work in pairs. Replace the words in purple in Exercise 7 with these words. Act out the conversation.

> What time is it?

> It's a quarter past eight.

1 eleven o'clock / five past eleven / half past eleven

2 English / geography / science / math

3 twelve o'clock / twenty-five past twelve / twelve forty-five

4 twelve forty-five / one o'clock / one thirty

9 Act out the conversation again with your own words and ideas.

Grammar • Present simple: questions and short answers

Questions		
Do I/you/we/they	get up	at seven o'clock?
Does he/she/it	get up	
Short answers		
Yes, I/you/we/they do. No, I/you/we/they don't.		
Yes, he/she/it does. No, he/she/it doesn't.		

Grammar reference page 112

1 Study the grammar table. Complete the rules.

1 Present simple questions start with *Do* or ..... .
2 Short answers with *Yes* end with *do* or ..... .
3 Short answers with *No* end with *don't* or ..... .

2 Choose the correct options to make questions. Then write answers.

1 *Do / Does* Nick and Monica get up early?
   Do Nick and Monica get up early? Yes, they do.
2 *Do / Does* they go to the same school?
3 *Do / Does* Monica walk to school?
4 *Do / Does* Monica live on a farm?
5 *Do / Does* Nick have history first?

3 Make questions for these answers.

1 No, I don't speak German.
   Do you speak German?
2 No, we don't live in Houston.
3 Yes, she goes to school by bus.
4 Yes, we write essays in English.
5 No, I don't. I have lunch at 2 p.m.
6 Yes, he studies French.

4 Make questions. In pairs, ask and answer.

1 you / get up / at half past six?
   Do you get up at half past six? No, I don't.
2 you / go to school / at 7:15?
3 your friend / like / math?
4 your teacher / watch TV / after school?
5 you and your family / have dinner together?
6 you / go to bed / at ten thirty?
7 your friends / bike to school?

Reading

1 Look quickly at the quiz. Can you find this information?

1 Eight countries.
2 The names of two schools.

The Big School Quiz

Do you know about schools in other countries?
Take this quiz and find out!

1 The City Montessori School in Lucknow, India, is very big. How many students study there?
a 12,000
b 22,000
c More than 39,000

2 In France, some students never go to school on …
a Saturdays and Sundays.
b Wednesdays and Sundays.
c Sundays and Mondays.

3 In Sweden, Switzerland and Denmark, some children start school at …
a 7 years old.
b 8 years old.
c 9 years old.

4 In South Korea, some students stay at school after classes end at 4 p.m. Do they …
a do their homework?
b clean up their classrooms?
c watch TV?

5 Australian children go to school 200 days a year. How many days a year do Chinese children go to school?
a 211 days a year
b 231 days a year
c 251 days a year

6 Shishi Middle School in China is about …
a one thousand years old.
b three thousand years old.
c two thousand years old.

7 In China, some children finish school at …
a 12 years old.
b 15 years old.
c 16 years old.

Answer key

1 c 2 b 3 a 4 a 5 c 6 c 7 b

Key Words

find out   to stay   thousand

2 Take the quiz. Then listen and check your answers.
1.41

3 Now read about your score.

0 – 2 Uh oh! Find out about other countries.
3 – 5 Well done. You know some interesting facts.
6 – 7 Excellent!

4 Read the quiz again. Name the countries.
1.41
1 There is a 2,000-year-old school in this country.
China
2 The school day ends at 4 p.m. in this country.
3 The City Montessori School is in this country.
4 Children go to school for 200 days a year in this country.
5 Students can finish school when they are 15 in this country.
6 Some children start school at 7 years old in these three countries.

Listening

1 Listen to an interview. Put the topics in order 1–3.
1.42
a summer
b clothes
c break

2 Listen again. Correct the sentences.
1.42
1 Jin goes to school in Japan.
2 His school day ends at 4 p.m.
3 He has one hour for his lunch break.
4 He wears a blue shirt and blue pants.
5 He exercises on Monday and Thursday.
6 He doesn't study in summer.

3 Listen again. Swap books and check
1.42 **your partner's answers.**

Writing • An email

1 Read the Writing File.

> **Writing File**   Time phrases
>
> **We use these words to make time phrases:**
> - on + day
> - in + *the morning* / *the afternoon*
> - at + time

2 Read the email. Find time phrases with *on*, *in* and *at*.

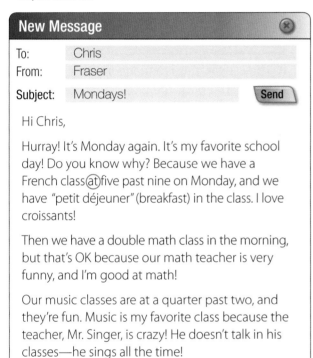

> **New Message** ⊗
>
> To: Chris
> From: Fraser
>
> Subject: Mondays!   **Send**
>
> Hi Chris,
>
> Hurray! It's Monday again. It's my favorite school day! Do you know why? Because we have a French class at five past nine on Monday, and we have "petit déjeuner" (breakfast) in the class. I love croissants!
>
> Then we have a double math class in the morning, but that's OK because our math teacher is very funny, and I'm good at math!
>
> Our music classes are at a quarter past two, and they're fun. Music is my favorite class because the teacher, Mr. Singer, is crazy! He doesn't talk in his classes—he sings all the time!
>
> What about you? Do you like Mondays?
>
> Bye for now,
>
> Fraser

3 Read the email again. Answer the questions.

1 Does Fraser like Mondays? *Yes, he does.*
2 What time is Fraser's French class?
3 Does Fraser have math on Mondays?
4 Is Fraser good at math?
5 Who is Fraser's music teacher?
6 What does the music teacher do?

4 Choose the correct options.

1 I have English *in* / *at* the morning.
2 Our art class is *at* / *on* Friday.
3 My school day starts *in* / *at* eight o'clock.
4 We have PE *in* / *on* the afternoon.

5 Think about your favorite school day. Answer the questions.

1 What is your favorite day?
2 What classes do you have on your favorite day?
3 Who are your teachers? What subjects do they teach?
4 What time are your classes?
5 What is your favorite class?

6 Write a short email about your favorite school day. Use "My email" and your answers from Exercise 5.

> **My email** ⊗
>
> 1 Start your email.
>   *Dear/Hi … ,*
> 2 Say what your favorite day is.
>   *My favorite day is … .*
> 3 Say what classes you have.
>   *We have … on … .*
> 4 Say who your teachers are and what subjects they teach.
> 5 Say what time your classes are.
> 6 Say what your favorite class is and why.
>   *… is my favorite class because … .*
> 7 Finish your email.
>   *See you soon! / Bye for now!*

> **Remember!**
> - Use time phrases to describe when things happen.
> - Use the Present simple.
> - Use the vocabulary in this unit.
> - Check your grammar, spelling and punctuation.

Refresh Your Memory!

Grammar • Review

1 **Make sentences. Use the Present simple affirmative.**

1 Linda / watch / TV before school.
   Linda watches TV before school.
2 Max / study / French / in college.
3 Eva and Sara / study / math.
4 My dad / clean up / the house every evening.
5 My brother / play / soccer in the backyard.
6 You / get up / before me.

2 **Complete the sentences with the Present simple negative.**

1 I get up early, but Adam .... .
   I get up early, but Adam *doesn't get up early.*
2 You like history, but Nadia .... .
3 I have lunch at school, but Mom and Dad .... .
4 We walk to school, but Maria and Anna .... .
5 I go to bed at 10 p.m., but my sister .... .
6 I do my homework in front of the TV, but you .... .

3 **Complete the email with *do*, *don't*, *does* or *doesn't*.**

Hi Marta,

What subjects ¹ *do* you study at school? We can choose subjects now because we are fourteen. I ² .... have history classes now, but I study geography. I ³ .... study art because I can't paint. My friend Matt ⁴ .... like French, so his language class is German. ⁵ .... your school give you a choice? At what age ⁶ .... you choose? Write and tell me!

Veronica

4 **Match the questions to the correct answers.**

1 Does Alan like dogs? *b*
2 Do you walk to school?
3 Do I start school before you?
4 Do Pepe and Nina read books in English?
5 Does Angela meet her friends before school?

a Yes, they do.
b No, he doesn't.
c Yes, she does.
d Yes, I do.
e No, you don't.

Vocabulary • Review

5 **Complete the routine verbs.**

Dan gets ¹ *up* at 6 every morning. He doesn't ² .... dressed or ³ .... his teeth, and he doesn't ⁴ .... a shower. He ⁵ .... breakfast, but he doesn't ⁶ .... TV, and he doesn't ⁷ .... homework. He ⁸ .... to bed when he wants to. Why? Because Dan is my dog!

6 **Match the definitions to these words.**

art	computer science	English	~~French~~
geography	literature	music	PE

1 They speak this language in France. *French*
2 We learn about the world and other countries in this class.
3 We play soccer and basketball in this class.
4 This class teaches us about books, stories and poems.
5 We paint pictures in this class.
6 We learn about computers in this class.
7 They speak this language in the US.
8 We play instruments in this class.

Speaking • Review

7 1.43 **Put the sentences in the correct order. Then listen and check.**

a It starts at eleven fifteen. We're early.
b What time is it? *1*
c What time does it end?
d Oh. What time is our French class?
e It ends at twelve twenty.
f It's ten ten.

Dictation

8 1.44 **Listen and write in your notebook.**

9 **Swap books and check your partner's work.**

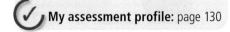
My assessment profile: page 130

Technology File

How to Make a Camera Obscura

What you need ...

- a tube – for example, an old chips tube
- a ruler
- scissors
- some aluminum foil
- a needle
- some adhesive tape
- some black paint and a paintbrush
- tracing paper
- two big rubber bands

1 Eat the chips! Then clean the inside of the tube and paint it black inside and outside.

2 Draw a line around the tube 5 cm from the bottom. Then cut along the line. You now have two tubes—one short tube and one long tube.

3 With the needle, make a hole at the bottom of the short tube.

4 Tape some tracing paper on the top of the short tube. Then tape the short tube and the long tube together again. The tracing paper is now in the middle of the tube.

5 Put the aluminum foil all around the tube and attach with rubber bands.

6 Go outside. Close one eye. Put the tube over the other eye. Hold your hand up to the sky and point the tube at it.

7 The light comes through the pinhole and makes a color image on the tracing paper. What is strange about the image?

Reading

1 Read the text quickly. Put the pictures in the correct order.

1 *b*

2 Read the text again. Answer the questions.

1.45

1 What color do you paint the tube? *black*

2 Do you cut around the top or the bottom of the tube?

3 How do you make the hole in the tube?

4 What do you put around the tube?

5 How do you look through the camera?

6 Where do you see the image when you use a Camera Obscura?

My Technology File

3 In pairs, make a Camera Obscura.

4 Write two sentences about the image on the tracing paper.

Grammar • Have

1 **Complete the sentences with *has* or *have*.**

1 He *has* seven brothers.
2 They .... a black-and-white dog.
3 It .... big teeth.
4 I .... my cell phone.
5 She .... a big house.
6 We .... a good French teacher.

2 **Put the sentences in Exercise 1 in the negative.**

1 *He doesn't have seven brothers.*

3 **Complete the conversation.**

A ¹ *Do* you ² .... a TV in your bedroom?
B No, I ³ .... , but I ⁴ .... a laptop. I watch my sister's DVDs on it.
A ⁵ .... your sister have a lot of DVDs?
B Yes, she ⁶ .... , but she doesn't ⁷ .... the new Robert Pattinson movie.
A ⁸ .... they have it in stores now?
B Yes, they ⁹ .... . I love Robert Pattinson!

• Possessive 's

4 **Copy the sentences. Add an apostrophe in the correct place.**

1 My dad's shoes are horrible.
2 Her sisters names are Kate and Lianne.
3 This towns shopping mall is boring.
4 I like Sams parents.
5 They're Stan and Sophies friends.
6 All the teachers cars are in front of the school.

• Possessive adjectives

5 **Complete the second sentence so it has a similar meaning to the first sentence.**

1 I have a green bag.
   My bag is green.
2 She has an interesting book.
   .... book is interesting.
3 It has awesome pictures.
   .... pictures are awesome.
4 They have a good camera.
   .... camera is good.

• There is/There are; Some/Any

6 **Complete the questions about Allendale. Then answer them using the information from the table.**

1 Are there any houses? *Yes, there are.*
2 .... a post office? .... .
3 .... any banks? .... .
4 .... a movie theater? .... .
5 .... a park? .... .
6 .... any schools? .... .

WHAT'S IN ALLENDALE?			
houses	800	stores	4
schools	2	lakes	✗
banks	✗	a museum	✓
a park	✓	cafés	6
a post office	✓	a sports complex	✗
a movie theater	✗	a library	✗

7 **The information in this paragraph is not correct. Rewrite the paragraph correctly.**

There aren't any stores in Allendale, but there are some lakes. There are some museums, and there's a café. There's a sports complex, and there's a library.
There are some stores in Allendale, but ... .

• Can/Can't for ability

8 **Make sentences with *can/can't*.**

1 I / climb / trees / ✓
   I can climb trees.
2 My dad / dance / ✗
3 My friends / juggle / ✓
4 You / skate / ✗
5 We / bike / to school / ✓
6 The baby / walk / ✗

9 **Make questions. Then answer.**

1 Lady Gaga / sing / Can / ?
   Can Lady Gaga sing? Yes, she can.
2 dogs / fly / Can / ?
3 you / Can / in English / write / ?
4 Can / run / fast / good soccer players / ?

• Present simple

10 **Complete the text with the Present simple form of the verbs.**

I ¹ *live* (live) in Australia. My home is 200 km from a town, so I ² .... (not go) to school every day. I ³ .... (have) classes on the Internet. My brother ⁴ .... (not live) at home from Monday to Friday. He ⁵ .... (stay) at his school, and we only ⁶ .... (see) him on the weekend. After his classes, he ⁷ .... (study) with his friends.

11 **Look at the information. Then complete the sentences.**

On Fridays at …	4 o'clock	5 o'clock	6 o'clock
Maria and Dan	play soccer	do homework	meet friends
Jacob	clean up the classroom	go to the park	have dinner

1 Maria and Dan *don't meet* friends at 4 o'clock.
2 Jacob .... the classroom at 4 o'clock.
3 Maria and Dan .... homework at 5 o'clock.
4 Jacob .... to the park at 6 o'clock.
5 Maria and Dan .... soccer at 6 o'clock.

12 **Make questions. Then answer using the information from Exercise 11.**

1 Jacob / have dinner / at 5 o'clock / ?
Does Jacob have dinner at 5 o'clock?
No, he doesn't.
2 he / clean up the classroom / at 4 o'clock / ?
3 Maria and Dan / play soccer / at 6 o'clock / ?
4 they / go to the park / at 5 o'clock / ?
5 Jacob / do homework / at 6 o'clock / ?

13 **Make questions.**

1 No, I don't. (have breakfast at school)
Do you have breakfast at school?
2 Yes, we do. (walk to school)
3 No, she doesn't. (read a lot of books)
4 Yes, it does. (start at half past nine)
5 No, I don't. (get up at six o'clock)

Speaking • Talking about position

1 **Look at the picture and complete the sentences with these words.**

| behind | in | in front of | next to | ~~on~~ | under |

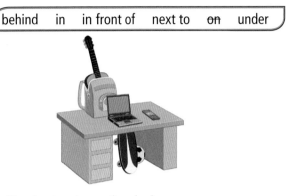

1 The laptop is *on* the desk.
2 The cell phone is .... the laptop.
3 The backpack is .... the laptop.
4 The guitar is .... the backpack.
5 The ball is .... the desk.
6 The skateboard is .... the ball.

• Orders and warnings

2 **Match the beginnings (1–5) to the endings (a–e) of the teacher's instructions.**

1 Open   a down!
2 Stand   b your books.
3 Be   c quiet!
4 Sit   d up!
5 Don't   e shout in class.

• Time

3 **Make questions. Then look at the clocks and write the answers.**

1 does / What time / start / it / ?
What time does it start?
It starts at a quarter to four/three forty-five.
2 is / time / What / it / ?
3 end / time / What / it / does / ?

Vocabulary • Objects

1 Complete the sentences with these words.

DVD	game console	~~guitar~~
laptop	magazines	MP3 player
posters	wallet	watch

1 My brother can play the *guitar*. He's very good!
2 I read a lot of .... .
3 I don't have a .... . What time is it?
4 Do you do your homework on a .... ?
5 Do you have any good music on your .... ?
6 I only have one dollar in my .... .
7 Can you play *MotorMania* on that .... ?
8 I have ten .... on my bedroom walls.
9 Can we watch a .... ?

• Adjectives

2 Complete the words.

1 He's a g o o d actor, but I don't like his movies.
2 A lot of people play soccer. It's very p_ _ _ar.
3 You can do today's homework in 15 minutes. It's e_ _ _ .
4 What?! $35 for a pen?! That's very e_ _ _ns_ _ _.
5 Our car's very o_ _, but we like it.
6 She has a sm_ _ _ dog in her bag. Look!
7 I play tennis, but I'm a very b_ _ player.
8 That watch is very ch _ _ _, only $5.
9 Don't watch that DVD. It's b_ _ i _ _.
10 Her classes are very in_ _ _ _ _ _ _ng.

• Places in a town

3 Match the beginnings (1–8) to the endings (a–h) of the sentences.

1 Send a letter at — a the bank.
2 You can see old things at — b the movie theater.
3 You can find new clothes at
4 There are a lot of dollars at — c the shopping mall.
5 You can eat at
6 Dogs and people walk in — d the post office.
7 There are a lot of books at — e the museum.
8 You can watch movies at — f the café.
g the park.
h the library.

• Action verbs

4 Complete the sentences with these words.

| bike | climb | fly | juggle |
| jump | play | run | ~~walk~~ |

1 My friends *walk* to school.
2 I .... to school on my mountain bike.
3 My grandma can .... ten kilometers.
4 My grandpa can .... six balls.
5 People often .... to Greece on vacation.
6 I can't .... soccer.
7 She can .... very high.
8 Can you .... this tree?

• Daily routines

5 Complete the sentences with these words.

bed	breakfast	brush	clean up
dinner	dressed	~~get~~	go
homework	lunch	meet	shower
start	watch		

I ¹ *get* up at seven o'clock. Then I get ² .... in my school uniform, have ³ .... (eggs and toast!) and ⁴ .... my teeth. I ⁵ .... school at nine o'clock. I have ⁶ .... at school. After school, I ⁷ .... my friends in the park. Next, I ⁸ .... home, do all my ⁹ .... and ¹⁰ .... TV. Then I have ¹¹ .... . My favorite is pizza! I take a ¹² .... after that. Then I ¹³ .... my room and go to ¹⁴ .... .

• School subjects

6 Complete the school subjects.

1 m a t h
2 m u _ _ _
3 F _ _ _ c h
4 E _ _ _ _ s h
5 h _ s t _ _ _
6 s c _ _ n _ _
7 l i t _ _ _ t u r e
8 g _ _ g r _ _ _ y
9 c _ _ _ _ _er sc _ _ _ c _

Word list

Unit 1 • My World

Objects

camera	/ˈkæmərə/
cell phone	/ˈsɛl foʊn/
comics	/ˈkɑmɪks/
DVD	/diːviˈdiː/
game console	/ˈgeɪm ˈkɑnsoʊl/
guitar	/gɪˈtɑr/
ice skates	/ˈaɪs skeɪts/
laptop	/ˈlæptɑp/
magazine	/ˌmægəˈzin/
MP3 player	/ɛmpi θri ˈpleɪər/
poster	/ˈpoʊstər/
skateboard	/ˈskeɪtbɔrd/
wallet	/ˈwɑlɪt/
watch	/wɑtʃ/

Adjectives

bad	/bæd/
big	/bɪg/
boring	/ˈbɔrɪŋ/
cheap	/tʃip/
difficult	/ˈdɪfɪkəlt/
easy	/ˈizi/
expensive	/ɪkˈspɛnsɪv/
good	/gʊd/
interesting	/ˈɪntrɪstɪŋ, ˈɪntəˌrɛstɪŋ/
new	/nu/
old	/oʊld/
popular	/ˈpɑpyələr/
small	/smɔl/
unpopular	/ʌnˈpɑpyələr/

Unit 2 • Around Town

Places in a town

bank	/bæŋk/
bus station	/ˈbʌs ˈsteɪʃən/
café	/kæˈfeɪ/
hospital	/ˈhɑspɪtl/
library	/ˈlaɪbrɛri/
movie theater	/ˈmuvi ˈθiətər/
museum	/mjuːˈziːəm/
park	/pɑrk/
police station	/pəˈlis ˈsteɪʃən/
post office	/ˈpoʊst ˈɔfɪs/
shopping mall	/ˈʃɑpɪŋ mɔl/
sports complex	/ˈspɔrts ˌkɑmplɛks/
town square	/ˈtaʊn ˈskwɛr/
train station	/ˈtreɪn ˈsteɪʃən/

Action verbs

bike	/baɪk/
climb	/klaɪm/
dance	/dæns/
fly	/flaɪ/
juggle	/ˈdʒʌgəl/
jump	/dʒʌmp/
play	/pleɪ/
run	/rʌn/
sing	/sɪŋ/
skate	/skeɪt/
swim	/swɪm/
walk	/wɔk/

Unit 3 • School Days

Daily routines

brush my teeth	/ˈbrʌʃ maɪ ˈtiθ/
clean up my room	/ˈklin ʌp maɪ ˈrum/
do homework	/ˈdu ˈhoʊmwərk/
get dressed	/ˈget ˈdrɛst/
get up	/ˈget ʌp/
go home	/ˈgoʊ ˈhoʊm/
go to bed	/ˈgoʊ tə ˈbɛd/
have breakfast	/ˈhæv ˈbrɛkfəst/
have dinner	/ˈhæv ˈdɪnər/
have lunch	/ˈhæv ˈlʌntʃ/
meet friends	/ˈmit ˈfrɛndz/
start school	/ˈstɑrt ˈskul/
take a shower	/ˈteɪk ə ˈʃaʊər/
watch TV	/ˈwatʃ ˌtiˈvi/

School subjects

art	/ɑrt/
computer science	/kəmˈpyutər ˈsaɪəns/
English	/ˈɪŋglɪʃ/
French	/frɛntʃ/
geography	/dʒiˈɑgrəfi/
history	/ˈhɪstəri/
literature	/ˈlɪtərətʃər/
math	/ˈmæθ/
music	/ˈmyuzɪk/
PE	/piˈi/
science	/ˈsaɪəns/
social studies	/ˈsoʊʃəl ˈsaɪəns/

4 Animal Magic

Grammar
Adverbs of frequency;
Present simple with *Wh*
questions; *Must/Mustn't*

Vocabulary
Unusual animals;
Parts of the body

Speaking
Likes and dislikes

Writing
An animal fact sheet

Word list page 57
Workbook page 119

Vocabulary • Unusual animals

1 Match the pictures to these words. Then listen, check and repeat.

2.1

> frog
> giant rabbit
> hissing cockroach
> lizard
> parrot *1*
> piranha
> pygmy goat
> python
> stick insect
> tarantula

2 Find one animal in Exercise 1 for each of these categories. Then think of two more.

1 fish *piranha*, ... ,
2 spider
3 bird
4 amphibian
5 reptile
6 mammal
7 insect

3 In pairs, read the clues and guess the animal.

1 It can fly. *a bird*
2 It's green. It lives in water. It eats insects.
3 It can swim, but it can't walk.
4 It lives under the ground. It eats vegetables. It's a popular pet.
5 It makes a loud noise. It's an insect.
6 It can't walk, and it can't fly, but it can climb trees.
7 People drink its milk.
8 It can say words.

4 Think of an animal. In pairs, ask and answer.

Can it fly?

Yes, it can.

Is it a parrot?

Yes, it is.

Brain Trainer
Activity 4
Go to page 61

Reading

1 Look at the photos. What do you think the text is about?

a An article about tarantulas.
b A text about life in a zoo.
c A blog about animals.

2 Read the text and check your answers to Exercise 1.

3 Read the text again. Answer the questions.

2.2
1 What's Tom's job? *He's a zookeeper.*
2 When does Tom get up?
3 When does he start work?
4 Where do the hissing cockroaches come from?
5 Where does the tarantula come from?
6 What animals is Tom scared of?
7 What does Tom think about his job?

4 Read the text again. Are the statements true (T) or false (F)?

2.2
1 Tom feeds the animals in the morning. *F*
2 Tom sometimes hides the hissing cockroaches' food in different places.
3 Tiny is only ten years old.
4 Visitors to the zoo are scared of the red-knee tarantula.
5 Tom enjoys his job because he can learn more about animals.
6 Tom isn't tired at the end of the day.

5 What about you? In pairs, ask and answer.
1 Which animals do you like/dislike?
2 What unusual animals do you know of?
3 Are you scared of spiders or insects?

> Do you like animals?

> I love animals, but I'm scared of reptiles.

A Day in the Life ...

Tom works in the Unusual Pets section of Bemidji Animal Park in Minnesota. He is a zookeeper. We talk to him about a typical day.

Describe a typical day at the zoo.

I get up at 6:30, and I start work at 8 o'clock. I usually put on my boots because it's often very dirty in the animal enclosures. I clean the animal enclosures every day, and in the afternoon I feed the animals. I'm always busy! I never finish work before 5:30.

What animals do you like, and what animals do you dislike?

I love the hissing cockroaches! They come from Madagascar, and they're very noisy. I sometimes hide their food in different places. It's a game for them! But I don't like the tarantulas. We have a red-knee tarantula from Mexico. Her name's Tiny, and she's twenty-five years old. Visitors to the zoo love her, but I'm scared of spiders. I hardly ever work with them.

Why do you like your job?

I work with great people, and I learn new things about animals every day. At the end of the day, I'm often tired, but my job is always interesting.

Grammar • Adverbs of frequency

0% 10%	25% 50%	80% 100%
never / hardly ever	sometimes / often	usually / always
I hardly ever work with them.	I'm often very tired.	My job is always interesting.

1 Study the grammar table. Choose the correct options to complete the rule.

> Adverbs come *before* / *after* the verb *to be* and *before* / *after* most other verbs.

2 Put the adverbs in the correct place.

1 We go to the zoo on the weekend. (sometimes)
  We sometimes go to the zoo on the weekend.
2 My English class is interesting. (usually)
3 My parrot watches TV in the morning. (often)
4 My dad is happy on Friday evening. (always)
5 I bike to school. (never)
6 You take our dog for a walk. (hardly ever)

3 Put the words in the correct order to make sentences.

1 often / Tom / very / is / tired / work / After
  After work Tom is often very tired.
2 trees / sometimes / Goats / climb
3 eighteen / Cats / sleep / often / hours / for
4 after / feed / rabbit / my / usually / I / school
5 ever / Sarah / her / hardly / parrot / talks / to

4 Look at the chart and complete the sentences.

On the weekend	Peter	Abby
1 play soccer	100%	50%
2 play computer games	80%	10%
3 do homework	80%	100%
4 listen to music	0%	80%

1 Peter *always* plays soccer on the weekend.
  Abby *often plays soccer on the weekend.*
2 Peter .... plays computer games on the weekend.
  Abby .... .
3 Peter .... does his homework on the weekend.
  Abby .... .
4 Peter .... listens to music on the weekend.
  Abby .... .

• Present simple with *Wh* questions

Wh questions	
Where do you live?	In Manchester.
When do you finish school?	At four o'clock.
What does she eat for breakfast?	Cereal.
Who does Mrs. West teach?	8th grade students.
Why do you walk to school?	Because we don't have a car.
How often do you play football?	Every day!

Grammar reference page 114

5 Study the grammar table. Choose the correct options to complete the rules.

> 1 We use *who* to ask about *people* / *things*.
> 2 We use *what* to ask about *people* / *things*.
> 3 We use *when* to ask about *place* / *time*.
> 4 We use *where* to ask about *place* / *time*.

6 Match the questions to the answers.

1 How often do elephants eat?
2 Who is your favorite singer?
3 When is your birthday?
4 What is in your schoolbag?
5 Why do you take the bus?
6 Where do piranhas live?

a Ariana Grande.
b It's on June 17.
c Because we don't have a car.
d They live in South American rivers.
e They eat every three hours.
f Two pens, a ruler and a book about spiders.

7 What about you? Make questions. In pairs, ask and answer.

Where do you live?   I live in San Jose.

1 Where / you / live?
2 Who / your / best friend?
3 How often / you / play sports?
4 What / your / favorite animal?
5 What / you / usually / do / on the weekend?
6 How often / you / go / to the zoo?

Vocabulary • Parts of the body

1 Label the picture with these words. Then listen, check and repeat.

2.3

arm	beak 1	fin	finger	foot	hand	head
leg	neck	paw	tail	toe	wing	

Word list page 57
Workbook page 119

2 What parts of the body do we have? Complete the sentences with words from Exercise 1.

1 We have **zero** *tails*.
2 We have **one** .... .
3 We have **two** .... .
4 We have **ten** .... .

3 What animal is it? Read the clues and guess.

bird	~~fish~~	pygmy goat	hissing cockroach	spider

1 It doesn't have legs. It has a head. It doesn't have arms. It has fins. *It's a fish.*
2 It has six legs. It has a head. It doesn't have a neck.
3 It has eight legs. It doesn't have a tail.
4 It has two legs. It has a tail. It doesn't have arms. It has wings and a beak.
5 It has four legs and a tail. It doesn't have fins.

4 Complete the descriptions with these words. Then listen and check.

2.4

beak	bird	eyes	head
insects	~~legs~~	tail	wings

The wolf spider is an unusual pet. It has eight ¹ *legs*, and it can run and jump. It also has eight ² .... , and it can see in the dark. The wolf spider's ³ .... is small, but its body is large. It eats ⁴ .... .

A cockatiel is a ⁵ .... . It has a yellow, gray or white head, with a small ⁶ .... . Its ⁷ .... are usually gray and white, and it has a long black or gray ⁸ .... . Cockatiels are from Australia, but they are popular pets around the world.

Brain Trainer
Activity 5
Go to page 61

Chatroom Likes and dislikes

Speaking and Listening

1 Look at the photos. **Answer the questions.**

1 Where are the children?
2 What animals can you see?
3 Do you think Nick is angry or happy?

2 Listen and read the conversation. **Are the**
2.5 **statements true (T) or false (F)?**

1 Sunny mustn't be on a leash on the farm. *F*
2 Sunny doesn't like running around the farm.
3 Monica likes living on a farm.
4 Monica likes getting up early.
5 Leo doesn't like getting up early.
6 Leo wants to feed the animals.
7 Monica's goats don't like eating Sunny's leash.

3 Act out the conversation in groups of four.

Monica	Hi, guys! Nick, you must put Sunny on a leash, please.
Nick	Sorry, Monica. Sunny loves running around the farm.
Julia	Do you like living on a farm, Monica?
Monica	Yes, I do, but I hate getting up early in the morning.
Leo	Me too! I don't like getting up early either.
Julia	That's true! On the weekend, you don't get up before 11!
Leo	I love feeding the animals. Look! I have some candy for them.
Monica	No, don't give them unhealthy food, Leo.
Leo	Sorry!
Nick	Sunny! Come here. You mustn't run away.
Monica	That's strange. Where's Sunny's leash?
Nick	I don't know.
Julia	Monica, what do your goats like eating?
Monica	They like eating everything!
Leo	Look! They love eating Sunny's leash!

Say it in your language …
Hi, guys!
Me too!

4 Look back at the conversation. Find another way of saying …

1 *like* doing something
2 *don't like* doing something

5 Read the phrases for expressing likes and dislikes.

Likes	Dislikes
Sunny loves running around the farm.	I hate getting up early.
They like eating everything.	I don't like getting up early.

Pronunciation Contrastive stress

6a Listen. Which words are stressed?

2.6
1 **A** I love playing basketball.
   B Do you? I don't. I love playing computer games.
2 **A** Joe hates getting up early.
   B No, Joe loves getting up early. Emma hates getting up early.

b Listen again and repeat.
2.6

7 Listen to the conversations. Act out
2.7 the conversations in pairs.

Nick	I love ¹ watching animal shows on TV.
Julia	I don't.
Nick	I hate ² getting up early!
Julia	Me too!
Julia	I like ³ cooking!
Leo	I don't.

8 Work in pairs. Replace the words in purple in Exercise 7. Use these words and/or your own ideas. Act out the conversations.

I love watching TV.   Me too!

1 go to the movies / go to the theater

2 go to bed early / stay up late

3 sing / juggle

Grammar • Must/Mustn't

Affirmative
I/You/He/She/It/We/They must get up early.

Negative
I/You/He/She/It/We/They mustn't get up late.

Grammar reference page 114

1 Study the grammar table. Choose the correct option, 1 or 2, to complete the rule.

We use *must* and *mustn't* to talk about …
1 likes and dislikes.   2 important rules.

2 Choose *must* or *mustn't* for these school rules.

1 Students *must* / *mustn't* be late for school.
2 Students *must* / *mustn't* eat food in class.
3 Students *must* / *mustn't* listen to the teacher.
4 Students *must* / *mustn't* do their homework.
5 Students *must* / *mustn't* use cell phones in class.

3 Look at the farm notice. Make sentences with *you must* and *you mustn't*.

1 *You must be kind to the animals.*

Visitors to the Farm

✓	✗
1 Be kind to the animals	4 Hurt the animals
2 Close the gates	5 Give candy to the animals
3 Keep your dog on a leash	6 Climb the trees

Reading

1 Look at the text. Match the animals to their homes.

1 parrot   a tank
2 tarantula   b hutch
3 rabbit   c cage

Unusual Pets

This week three readers tell us about their unusual pets.

Boris has eight legs. His body is black, and his legs are black and white. He's a Costa Rican zebra tarantula from Central America. Boris eats small insects, and he lives in a tank with some twigs and pieces of wood. There's also a small box in his tank because Boris loves hiding. Spiders like hot, humid places, so Boris's tank is 22–30°C, and there's always a bowl of water there.
Lacey

My pet is a red-and-blue parrot. She's 25, but she isn't old. Parrots often live for 70 years! She's from Africa, and her name is Miki. She lives in a cage in my bedroom. Miki likes talking and singing songs. Parrots are friendly birds, and Miki loves being with people. When she sees my friends, she always says, "Hi, guys!"
Rashid

Clarence is a British giant rabbit. He weighs 7.5 kilos, and he eats a lot! He sleeps in a hutch in my bedroom. He loves playing under my bed, but sometimes he eats my socks. When he's in the backyard, he likes digging. His favorite food is grass, but he also loves eating carrots!
Katie

Key Words		
twig	to hide	humid
to weigh	to dig	grass

2 Read the text and check your answers to Exercise 1.

3 Read the text again. Write *Boris*, *Miki* or *Clarence*.
2.8
1 This pet likes hiding. *Boris*
2 This pet is red and blue.
3 This pet likes eating socks and carrots.
4 This pet eats insects.
5 This pet is sometimes outside.
6 This pet likes singing songs.

4 Read the text again. Answer the questions.
2.8
1 Where is Boris from?
Boris is from Central America.
2 Is Boris's tank hot or cold?
3 Is Miki old?
4 What does Miki say when she sees Rashid's friends?
5 How much does Clarence weigh?
6 Where does Clarence sleep?

Listening

1 Listen to the interview with Anna. Why is Dickens
2.9 a special dog?

2 Listen again. Answer the questions.
2.9
1 Name four things that Dickens does in the movie.
a He .... a tree.
b He .... out of a car.
c He .... in the ocean.
d He .... with a cat.
2 Who teaches Dickens?
3 What does he love doing?

3 Listen again. Swap books and check your
2.9 partner's answers.

Writing • An animal fact sheet

1 Read the Writing File.

2 Find the key information in this article. Is the same information in the fact sheet?

Komodo Dragons

Appearance

Komodo dragons are very big lizards. They grow to 3 meters and weigh 90 kilos. They are usually brown or gray in color, and they have a small head, a long tail and four short legs.

Habitat

Komodo dragons are from Indonesia. They live in deserts and in tropical regions.

Diet

Komodo dragons like eating birds, mammals—for example, goats and deer—or other reptiles.

Other Facts

Komodo dragons can run fast, and they can climb trees. They dig holes in the ground and sleep in them because they can stay cool there.

Komodo Dragon:
fact sheet

Color:	brown or gray
Length:	3 meters
Weight:	90 kilos
Country:	Indonesia
Habitat:	deserts and tropical regions
Diet:	birds, mammals, e.g., goats, deer, reptiles
Other facts:	can run fast & climb trees; dig holes & sleep in them – stay cool

3 Copy the sentences. Rewrite them as notes.

1 Komodo dragons have very strong legs, and they can climb trees.
   Komodo dragons v strong legs; can climb trees
2 Spiders eat insects. They catch them in their webs.
3 Snakes can't run or walk, but they can swim.

4 Read the fact sheet again. Answer the questions.

1 How heavy are Komodo dragons?
   They weigh 90 kilos.
2 What color are they?
3 What country do they come from?
4 What do they eat?
5 Where do they sleep?

5 Think of an unusual animal and take notes to complete the fact sheet.

My Unusual Animal
fact sheet

Color:	**Habitat:** ....
Length:	**Diet:** ....
Weight:	**Other facts:** ....
Country:	

6 Write a short article about your animal. Use the model from Exercise 2 and your notes from Exercise 5.

My unusual animal

1 Appearance
   They are ... . (color / length / weight)
2 Habitat
   They live in ... . (place / country)
3 Diet
   They eat ... . (animals / plants)
4 Other facts
   They can ... . (run / fly / swim / climb / jump)

Remember!
- Include the key information from your notes.
- Use the vocabulary in this unit.
- Check your grammar, spelling and punctuation.

Refresh Your Memory!

Grammar • Review

1 Copy and complete the frequency line with these adverbs.

always	hardly ever	~~never~~	often

0%	→	50%	→	100%
never	....	sometimes	....	usually	....

2 Put the words in the correct order to make sentences.

1 the / I / to / music / on / never / weekend / listen
   I never listen to music on the weekend.
2 o'clock / up / usually / get / at / You / seven
3 ever / We / grandparents / hardly / our / visit
4 talk / I / always / my / parrot / to
5 under / My / usually / the / sleeps / cat / bed

3 Read the answers. Complete the questions.

1 *Where* does your friend live?
   She lives in Seattle.
2 .... do you take your dog to the beach?
   Because he loves swimming in the ocean.
3 .... do you bike to school?
   Never. I don't have a bike.
4 .... is your favorite possession?
   My cell phone.
5 .... is your English teacher?
   My teacher is Ms. Clarkson.
6 .... do you have piano lessons?
   After school on Thursdays.

4 Complete the Pet Advice sheet with *You must* or *You mustn't*.

1 *You must feed your dog twice a day.*

Pet Advice: Dogs

1	✓	feed your dog twice a day
2	✓	take your dog for a walk every day
3	✓	give your dog a place to sleep
4	✗	give your dog unhealthy food—for example, chocolate
5	✗	shout at your dog
6	✓	keep your dog on a leash

Vocabulary • Review

5 Complete these unusual animal words with *a, e, i, o* and *u*.

1 h*i*ss*i*ng c*o*ckr*oa*ch
2 t_r_nt_l_
3 pygmy g_ _t
4 g_ _nt r_bb_t
5 fr_g

6 p_r_nh_
7 pyth_n
8 p_rr_t
9 l_z_rd
10 st_ck _ns_ct

6 Look at the animals from Exercise 5 again. Find …

1 four animals with four legs. *pygmy goat, …*
2 three animals with a tail.
3 two animals with six legs.
4 two animals with no legs.
5 one animal with two legs.
6 one animal with eight legs.

7 Complete the sentences with these words.

arms	beak	fingers	neck
paws	tail	toes	~~wings~~

1 My parrot can fly because she has *wings*.
   She eats her food with her .... .
2 My dog has four white .... and a black .... .
3 I have ten .... on my feet and ten .... on my hands.
4 Chimpanzees have two legs and two .... .
5 Giraffes have four long legs and a long .... .

Speaking • Review

8 Make sentences. Then listen and check.

2.10
Jim you / like / play / baseball?
     Do you like playing baseball?
Mike No, I don't. I like / watch / baseball on TV.
     you / like / watch / TV?
Jim No. I love / listen / to music and read / books,
     but I hate / watch TV.

Dictation

9 Listen and write in your notebook.

2.11

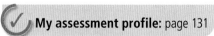
✓ **My assessment profile:** page 131

Real World Profiles

Lavindya's Profile

Age	Home country
6	India

City

Chennai

Reading

1 **Read Lavindya's profile. Are the statements true (T) or false (F)?**

1 Lavindya lives in the US.
2 She is ten years old.
3 She lives in Chennai.

2 **Read about Lavindya and her family.**
2.12 **Answer the questions.**

1 Where does Lavindya take a bath?
in a small pool outside
2 Why does she live at Arignar Anna Zoo?
3 How does she go to school?
4 What does she do in the afternoon?
5 What does she do when the elephants are tired?

Lavindya's Best Friend

It is seven o'clock in the morning in Chennai, southern India. Lavindya always takes her morning bath before school. But she doesn't take a bath at home. She takes a bath in a small pool outside with her best friend, a baby elephant!

Lavindya lives at Arignar Anna Zoo with her parents, brothers and sisters. Her father is a "mahout"—he works at the zoo, and he is a special keeper for the baby elephants. Lavindya is only six years old, but she can control the elephants, and she has a special friendship with them.

At eight o'clock in the morning, Lavindya goes to school, but she doesn't take the school bus. She rides an elephant to school. The elephant carries her backpack with its trunk. After school, Lavindya plays soccer with the elephants.

Now it is the evening, and the baby elephants are tired. Lavindya lies down next to them and pats their trunks. Sometimes they all sleep together—friends together in the day and friends together at night.

Class discussion

- Can you see elephants in your local zoo?
- How do you go to school in the morning?
- Think of three reasons why it's good to have a friendship with an animal.

Grammar • Adverbs of frequency

1 Make sentences about the people in the table with these adverbs.

Ella always gets up before 7 a.m.

~~always~~	hardly ever	never
often	sometimes	usually

I get up before 7 a.m.	Ella	Mia + Jade	Tom	Zak	Ali	Jo
Number of days in a year	365	2	70	150	0	351

2 Make sentences.

1 go home / They / at three thirty / usually
  They usually go home at three thirty.
2 often / is / late / She
3 hardly / eat pasta / I / ever
4 We / watch a DVD / on Fridays / always
5 at the café / are / sometimes / They / at 4:15
6 He / uses / his MP3 player / never

• Present simple with *Wh* questions

3 Make *Wh* questions for the answers with these words.

How often	What	~~When~~	Where	Who	Why

1 you / play tennis / ?
  At 4:30.
  When do you play tennis?
2 your grandparents / live / ?
  In Florida.
3 your favorite movie / ?
  Star Wars.
4 he / have PE classes / ?
  Every day.
5 Tom Cruise / ?
  He's an actor.
6 you / like / science / ?
  Because it's interesting.

• Must/Mustn't

4 Make sentences with *must* or *mustn't*.

1 they / have / breakfast / before 8 a.m.
  They must have breakfast before 8 a.m.
2 he / not / watch / TV / today
3 I / do / my math homework
4 she / brush / her teeth / every day
5 we / not / be / late for class

• Present continuous

5 Complete the sentences with the Present continuous of the verbs.

1 He*'s singing* (sing) his favorite song.
2 We .... (have) lunch at the moment.
3 They .... (not clean up) their bedroom.
4 She .... (run) to school because she's late.
5 You .... (not watch) TV.

6 Make questions and answers with the Present continuous.

1 they / use / the computer / ? ✗
  Are they using the computer? No, they aren't.
2 it / snow / at the moment / ? ✓
3 I / do / the correct exercise / ? ✓
4 you / bike / a long way / ? ✗
5 they / swim / in the ocean / ? ✗

• Present simple and Present continuous

7 Complete the conversation with the Present simple or Present continuous.

Luke Hi, Leah. What ¹ *are you doing* (you / do) at the train station?
Leah I ² .... (wait) for my friend Susan. She ³ .... (come) here for a week.
Luke That's great!
Leah Yes. I ⁴ .... (hardly ever / see) her because she ⁵ .... (swim) in competitions every weekend. What about you? Where ⁶ .... (you / go) now?
Luke To the beach.
Leah But it ⁷ .... (rain) today!
Luke I ⁸ .... (always / go) to the beach in the rain.

• Countable and uncountable nouns

8 **Are these words countable (C) or uncountable (U)?**

1 broccoli *U*   5 rice
2 egg   6 banana
3 sausage   7 tea
4 water   8 shrimp

9 **Choose the correct options.**

1 How *much / many* water do you have?
2 I'm eating *an / some* egg.
3 There isn't *much / many* juice in the fridge.
4 We have *a / some* bread.
5 Is there *much / many* shrimp in your pasta?

10 **Complete the conversation with these words.**

a	How many	How much	lot of
many	much	some (x2)	

A Let's make ¹*a* pizza!
B ² .... cheese do we have?
A We have a ³ .... cheese. We have ⁴ .... broccoli, too. We have ⁵ .... ham, but we don't have very ⁶ .... .
B ⁷ .... tomatoes do we have? I love pizzas with tomato sauce!
A We don't have ⁸ .... tomatoes. Just a few.
B OK. Let's put them on the pizza, too. Yum!

• Comparatives

11 **Write the comparative form of the adjectives.**

1 cold *colder*   6 clean
2 large   7 dirty
3 disgusting   8 good
4 noisy   9 hot
5 bad   10 horrible

12 **Make sentences with the comparative form of the adjective.**

1 your bag: 2012 / her bag: 2013 (new)
  Her bag is newer than your bag.
2 my math grade: C / my history grade: A (good)
3 Chicago: 5°C / Miami: 25°C (cold)
4 his parents: 50 / your parents: 39 (old)
5 surfing: $15 / horseback riding: $30 (expensive)

Speaking • Expressing likes and dislikes

1 **Make sentences.**

1 I / like / play / tennis
  I like playing tennis.
2 I / love / swim
3 my sister / love / ice skate
4 I / not like / do / sports
5 I / hate / be / in the water

2 **Complete the conversation with the sentences from Exercise 1.**

A ¹*I love swimming.*
B I don't. ² .... .
A What's your favorite sport?
B Well, tennis is fun. ³ .... with my sister in the summer. ⁴ .... with her friends in the winter, but I never go with them. ⁵ .... when it's cold.

• Expressing surprise

3 **Complete the words.**

1 **A** I got an email from Tammi. She's in Istanbul.
  B W <u>o w</u> !
2 **A** I _ove tarantulas.
  B R _ _ _ _ y?
3 **A** I have a ticket to the Olympic Games.
  B H _ w a _ _ z _ _ _!
4 **A** L _ _ k! That movie with Ashton Kutcher is on TV.
  B Gr _ _ _! He's my favorite actor.

• Ordering food

4 **Put the conversation in the correct order.**

Customer 1	Can I have a glass of apple juice, please?	....
Waiter	Are you ready to order?	*1*
Customer 1	Yes. I'd like the salmon and rice, please. What about you, Phil?	....
Waiter	Would you like anything to drink?	....
Customer 2	Me too!	....
Customer 1	It's delicious, thank you.	....
Waiter	How is your food?	....
Customer 2	I'll have the tuna salad, please.	....

Review 2

Vocabulary • Unusual animals

1 Fill in the missing letters in the words.

1 p y g _m_ _y_ g _o_ a t
2 t _ r _ n t _ _ a
3 p y _ _ o n
4 p i _ _ n _ a
5 h i _ _ i n g c _ _ k r _ _ c h
6 p _ _ r _ t
7 s _ _ c k i _ s _ _ t
8 f _ _ g
9 g i _ _ t r _ _ b _ t
10 l _ z _ _ d

• Parts of the body

2 Complete the sentences with these words.

arms	beak	fingers	foot	~~head~~	legs
neck	paw	tail	toes	wings	

1 A python has a small *head* and a long body.
2 A dog has four .... , but a stick insect has six.
3 A cat has a long .... .
4 A giraffe has a long .... .
5 We have ten .... and ten .... .
6 At the end of my leg is my .... .
7 At the end of our .... , we have hands.
8 A .... is the name for a dog's foot.
9 A parrot flies with its .... and eats with its .... .

• Activities

3 Match the descriptions to these words.

climbing	hiking
~~kayaking~~	mountain biking
painting	playing an instrument
horseback riding	singing
~~surfing~~	

1 You do this on water. *kayaking, surfing*
2 You do this at a music lesson.
3 You do this in art class.
4 You can do this in a tree.
5 You ride something in this activity.
6 You walk a long way in this activity.

• Weather and seasons

4 Read Meiko's diary. Complete the words.

• **January 10**
I love [1] win _t_ _e_ _r_ in Japan. It's very [2] c _ _ _.
Today it's [3] s _ _ _ ing. I can go skiing soon!

• **April 7**
In [4] sp _ _ _ _ we admire the pink flowers on
the cherry trees. It's [5] w _ _ m outside.

• **June 15**
It's [6] r _ _ n _ _ _ today. I don't like this weather!

• **July 27**
[7] S _ _ _ er is here! It's very [8] h _ _ and [9] su _ _ _.

• **October 2**
It's [10] au _ _ _ _. There are red leaves on the
trees. It's [11] cl _ _ d _ and [12] f _ _ _ y today.
It's very [13] w _ _ d _, too.

• Food and drinks

5 Put the words in the correct categories.

bananas	bread	broccoli	~~cheese~~
chicken	eggs	ham	juice
pasta	rice	salmon	sausage
shrimp	tea	tomatoes	tuna
water	yogurt		

1 Dairy *cheese*
2 Fish
3 Meat
4 Fruits and Vegetables
5 Drinks
6 Carbohydrates

• Adjectives

6 Complete the sentences with these words.

clean	~~delicious~~	dirty	disgusting
large	noisy	quiet	wonderful

1 I love this food. It's *delicious.*
2 Giant rabbits are very .... .
3 Be .... . Your brother's sleeping.
4 I hate cockroaches. They're .... .
5 I'm nice and .... after my shower.
6 I'm always .... after playing soccer.
7 That parrot talks a lot. It's very .... .
8 We're having a .... vacation. I love it here!

Word list

Unit 4 • Animal Magic

Unusual animals

frog	/frɔg/
giant rabbit	/ˈdʒaɪənt ˈræbɪt/
hissing cockroach	/ˈhɪsɪŋ ˈkɑk-roʊtʃ/
lizard	/ˈlɪzɚd/
parrot	/ˈpærət/
piranha	/pɪˈrɑnə/
pygmy goat	/ˈpɪgmi ˈgoʊt/
python	/ˈpaɪθɑn/
stick insect	/ˈstɪk ˈɪnsɛkt/
tarantula	/təˈræntʃələ/

Parts of the body

arm	/ɑrm/
beak	/bik/
fin	/fɪn/
finger	/ˈfɪŋgɚ/
foot	/fʊt/
hand	/hænd/
head	/hɛd/
leg	/lɛg/
neck	/nɛk/
paw	/pɔ/
tail	/teɪl/
toe	/toʊ/
wing	/wɪŋ/

Unit 5 • Out and About!

Activities

bowling	/ˈboʊlɪŋ/
climbing	/ˈklaɪmɪŋ/
dancing	/ˈdænsɪŋ/
gymnastics	/dʒɪmˈnæstɪks/
hiking	/ˈhaɪkɪŋ/
horseback riding	/ˈhɔrsbæk ˈraɪdɪŋ/
ice skating	/ˈaɪs ˈskeɪtɪŋ/
kayaking	/ˈkaɪækɪŋ/
mountain biking	/ˈmaʊntˀn ˈbaɪkɪŋ/
painting	/ˈpeɪntɪŋ/
playing an instrument	/ˈpleɪɪŋ ən ˈɪnstrəmənt/
rollerblading	/ˈroʊlɚˌbleɪdɪŋ/
singing	/ˈsɪŋɪŋ/
surfing	/ˈsɚfɪŋ/

Weather and seasons

autumn/fall	/ˈɔt əm/, /fɔl/
cloudy	/ˈklaʊdi/
cold	/koʊld/
foggy	/ˈfɑgi/
hot	/hɑt/
raining	/ˈreɪnɪŋ/
snowing	/ˈsnoʊɪŋ/
spring	/sprɪŋ/
summer	/ˈsʌmɚ/
sunny	/ˈsʌni/
warm	/wɔrm/
windy	/ˈwɪndi/
winter	/ˈwɪntɚ/

Unit 6 • Delicious!

Food and drinks

banana	/bəˈnænə/
bread	/brɛd/
broccoli	/ˈbrɑkəli/
cheese	/tʃiz/
chicken	/ˈtʃɪkən/
eggs	/ɛgz/
ham	/hæm/
juice	/dʒus/
pasta	/ˈpɑstə/
rice	/raɪs/
salmon	/ˈsæmən/
sausage	/ˈsɔsɪdʒ/
shrimp	/ʃrɪmp/
tea	/ti/
tomatoes	/təˈmeɪtoʊz/
tuna	/ˈtunə/
water	/ˈwɔt ɚ/
yogurt	/ˈyoʊgɚt/

Adjectives

clean	/klin/
cold	/koʊld/
delicious	/dɪˈlɪʃəs/
dirty	/ˈdɚti/
disgusting	/dɪsˈgʌstɪŋ/
horrible	/ˈhɔrəbəl/
hot	/hɑt/
large	/lɑrdʒ/
noisy	/ˈnɔɪzi/
quiet	/ˈkwaɪət/
small	/ˈsmɔl/
wonderful	/ˈwʌndɚfəl/

Brain Trainer

Find the difference

1 Look at the photo on page 14 for one minute. Now study this photo. What differences can you find?

Grammar

2 In pairs, look at the pictures. Then cover the pictures and choose A or B. Your partner reads the sentences. Correct them.

Paulo   Mike   Anya and Hans

Paulo has a magazine.
That's wrong. Mike has a magazine.

A
1 Paulo has a magazine.
2 Anya and Hans have skateboards.
3 Hans doesn't have a guitar.
4 Mike has a wallet.

B
1 Mike has a camera.
2 Hans has a watch.
3 Mike doesn't have an MP3 player.
4 Anya and Hans have backpacks.

Vocabulary

3a Complete the words. You have two minutes!

1 p _ s t e _   5 _ a l _ e t
2 _ a p _ o p   6 g _ i _ a _
3 c _ _ i c _   7 _ V _
4 _ a m e c _ n s o _ e   8 s k _ _ _ b _ _ _ d

3b Now make three more word puzzles for your partner to guess.

4 Work in pairs. Choose a numbered picture and say the adjective that matches it. Your partner finds the opposite adjective in the lettered pictures.

4. Easy.   C. Difficult.

Brain Trainer

Find the difference

1. Look at the photo on page 24 for one minute. Now study this photo. What differences can you find?

Grammar

2. Make true statements about your town or city using all the sentence beginnings below. Write the sentences in your notebook. You have two minutes!

In my town/city, there are … .

There's a … .

There isn't a … .

There are (two) … .

There aren't any … .

There are some … .

Vocabulary

3a. How many places in a town can you remember that have the letter *a* in them? Think of ten.

    1 *hospital*

3b. Label the places in the pictures.

    a *hospital*

a    f

b    g

c    h

d    i

e    j

4. Work in pairs. Choose six words from the list. Tell your partner what to do. Then switch roles.

bike	climb	dance	fly
juggle	jump	play	run
sing	skate	swim	walk

Walk (please) … .
(Now) jump … .

Brain Trainer

Find the difference

1. Look at the photo on page 34 for one minute. Now study this photo. What differences can you find?

Grammar

2. Make five sentences using all the words from the orange, purple and blue boxes.

   1 *I get up at 7 a.m.*

I	She	Sam	You	They

do homework	like	get up
goes to the movies	doesn't like	

math	after school	on Fridays
pizza	at 7 a.m.	

Vocabulary

3a. Read the phrases in the box aloud three times. Cover the box. Read the list below. Which phrase is missing?

   get up → take a shower → get dressed → have breakfast → start school → have lunch

   get up → take a shower → have breakfast → start school → have lunch

3b. Now try again.

   go home → do homework → meet friends → have dinner → watch TV → go to bed

   go home → do homework → meet friends → have dinner → go to bed

4a. Look at the books. What are the subjects?

   1 *art*

4b. Think of four subjects that are not in the pictures.

Brain Trainer

Find the difference

1 Look at the photo on page 48 for one minute. Now study this photo. What differences can you find?

Grammar

2 Add the correct *Wh* word to make questions. You have one minute!

1 *When* do you finish school?
2 .... is my guitar?
3 .... often do you go shopping?
4 .... is your favorite writer?
5 .... do you do after school?
6 .... do you have a camera today?

3 Make sentences with words of the same color. Then make your own color puzzle. In pairs, complete your partner's puzzle.

1 *I sometimes listen to music.*

I	soccer	usually	7 a.m.	She
to	sometimes	on	often	We
I	bikes	always	never	listen
Saturday	at	to	school	get up
He	watches	play	music	TV

Vocabulary

4a Complete the crossword.

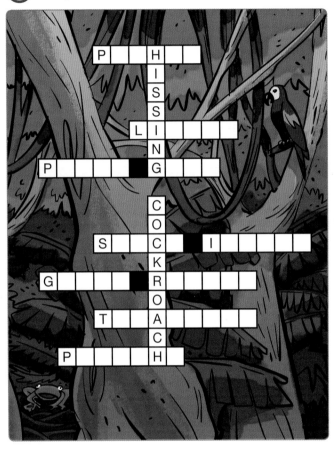

4b Two animals are missing from the puzzle. Can you name them?

5 Unscramble the words to complete the sentences with parts of the body. You have three minutes!

1 Parrots have **keabs** and **singw**.
   beaks and wings
2 Our cat has four big **waps** and a long **lait**.
3 We have ten **nerfsig** and **sote**.
4 My spider doesn't have **mars**, but it has eight **gels**.
5 Deer have small **hades** and long **skenc**.
6 Snakes don't have **teef** or **sahnd**. Sea snakes have **nifs**.

Reading

 1 Read the texts. Match the fact files (A–D) to the
3.41 correct state or city (1–4). Then listen and check.

2 Read the texts again. Answer the questions.
3.41
1 What language do most people speak
in the US?
2 Where are the following cities?
 a New York City   c Washington, DC
 b Los Angeles   d Chicago

Your culture

3 In pairs, answer the questions.
1 How many official languages are there
in your country?
2 What are the main ethnic groups?
3 Write a fact file for your country.
Include this information:
• location   • main cities
• population   • languages
• a fun fact about your region, city or town

The United States: Facts and Figures

The United States is made up of fifty
states. The federal government of the
US is in Washington, DC. The president
is the head of the executive branch of
the government. The other two branches
are Congress and the Supreme Court.
The United States is a multicultural
society. There is no official language,
but the vast majority of the people speak
English. There are many different ethnic
groups. People from all over the world live
in the US.

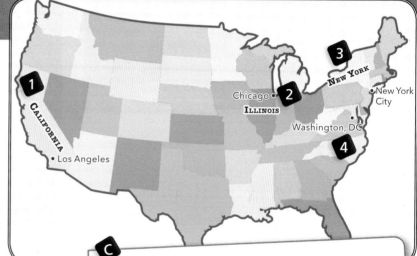

A
Location:	.... is in the midwest of the US.
Area:	149,998 km²
Population:	12.8 million
Capital:	Springfield
Main city:	Chicago
Fun fact:	The world's first skyscraper was built in Chicago in 1885.

B
Location:	.... is in the west of the US.
Area:	423,970 km²
Population:	38.8 million
Capital:	Sacramento
Main cities:	Los Angeles, San Diego, San Jose, San Francisco
Fun fact:	Frisbee, Barbie dolls and skateboards all come from this state.

C
Location:	...., is in the east of the US, between the states of Maryland and Virginia. It's the capital of the United States, and it has the status of a federal district.
Area:	177 km²
Population:	0.6 million
Fun fact:	Washington, DC, is the only city in the US that has a Spy Museum. It's a great place for James Bond fans!

D
Location:	.... is in the northeast of the US.
Area:	141,300 km²
Population:	19.7 million
Capital:	Albany
Main city:	New York City
Fun fact:	The first pizza place in the US opened in 1895 in New York City. Today some people say that New York pizza is the best pizza in the world!

Reading

1 Read the text. Answer the questions.

1 What are the three main stages of education in the US?
2 How many weeks of summer vacation do American students usually have?
3 Which exams do students take if they want to go to college?

2 Read the text again. Are these statements true (T) or false (F)?

1 Children go to elementary school from 6 to 11 years old.
2 The school year ends in August.
3 Students have lunch at school.
4 Education isn't free for children in the US.
5 American students wear a uniform in public schools.

Education stages

Name of school stage	Age
Elementary school	5–11 years old
Middle school	11–14 years old
High school	14–18 years old

The school year

The school year begins in late August or early September and ends in May or June. The main vacations are two weeks at Christmas, one or two weeks in spring and eight to twelve weeks in summer.

Interesting facts

- Education in the US is free for children 5 to 18 years old.
- In American public schools, most students do not wear a uniform, but students in some private schools wear them.
- Students call their teachers by their last name— for example, Mr. Brown or Ms. Jones.
- Most children go to public schools, but 10% go to private schools, and 3% are home-schooled.
- Students take standardized tests every year.
- In 11th grade, students take SAT or ACT exams for college admission.

Your culture

3 In pairs, answer the questions.

1 What are the main stages of education in your country?
2 Write a list of the main differences between your school and an American school. Think about uniforms, technology, vacations, subjects, school start and end times, exams and some interesting facts.

The school day

School usually starts at 8:30 or 9 a.m., and it gets out at 3 or 3:30 p.m. Students have lunch at school. They have their own "bag lunch" or a cooked school lunch. In elementary and middle school, students often have recess after lunch— free time to play outside or in the school gym.

Reading

1 Read the text quickly. Match the photos (A–D)
3.43 to each paragraph (1–4).

2 Read the text again. Answer the questions.
3.43
1 What do Americans eat for lunch?
2 Which meal do families usually
have together?
3 What kind of food is popular at Thanksgiving?
4 Describe a typical Sunday breakfast in the US.
5 When do people usually eat gingerbread?

Your culture

3 In pairs, answer the questions.
1 Do people have special meals on holidays
in your country? What do people cook
for holiday meals?
2 Describe a typical breakfast in your country.
Do people have a different breakfast
on the weekend?
3 When do people have their lunch in your
country? Is it a big meal, or do they have
a bag lunch?

1 Breakfast

People often have a quick breakfast of cereal,
milk, fruit and juice during the week.
On the weekends, people have eggs, bacon,
sausage, potatoes, toast and pancakes or
waffles for breakfast.

2 American lunch

People often have cold ham and cheese or
turkey sandwiches for lunch with potato chips
or fruit. Some Americans have fast food for
lunch, like hamburgers and French fries.

3 Dinner

Dinner is the traditional time for families
to eat together. They cook a main dish
like beef, pork or chicken and eat it with
potatoes or vegetables. Many people also have
Mexican, Italian or Chinese food for dinner.

4 Holiday meals

Most families have their Thanksgiving
or Christmas meals in the late afternoon.
At Thanksgiving, people usually have roast
turkey with cranberry sauce and pumpkin pie.
A typical Christmas dinner usually includes
roast beef, ham or goose, mashed potatoes,
fruitcake and gingerbread.

Meal times

In the US, the main meal times are:

Breakfast	7–9 a.m.
Lunch	12–2 p.m.
Dinner	6:30–8 p.m.

Dinner is usually the main meal of the day.

MOVE IT!

WORKBOOK WITH MP3S

SPLIT EDITION

1A

CHARLOTTE COVILL

SERIES CONSULTANT: CARA NORRIS-RAMIREZ

Contents

Starter Unit

Vocabulary • Countries and nationalities

1 **Write the countries and nationalities.**

Country	Nationality
¹ Spain	*Spanish*
²	English
France	³
Mexico	⁴
Greece	⁵
⁶	Brazilian

• Numbers

2 **Put the numbers in order. Write them below.**

eighteen	~~6~~	two hundred ninety-three
74	1,532	thirty-five

1 6   *six*
2 ....
3 ....
4 ....
5 ....
6 ....

• Spelling

3 **Listen and write the words.**

1 My name's *Kylie.*
2 I'm .... years old.
3 I'm from ....
4 We're at the .... Club Resort.
5 It's in ....

• Classroom objects

4 **Complete the crossword.**

Across

Down

• Days of the week and months of the year

5 Reorder the letters to make days of the week. Then write the days in the correct order.

1 aSudyn	*Sunday*	*Sunday*
2 Tesyuda	....	....
3 adFiry	....	....
4 yuTsrhda	....	....
5 yWaeddsne	....	....
6 traaudyS	....	....
7 yadnoM	....	....

6 Number the months in order.

February	☐	April	☐
June	☐	December	☐
November	☐	March	☐
October	☐	September	☐
July	☐	May	☐
January	1	August	☐

• Classroom language

7 Choose the one that doesn't belong.

1 November (Portugal) January February
2 book notebook May dictionary
3 Tuesday Spanish Greek Italian
4 pencil ruler eraser fifteen
5 interactive whiteboard fifteen forty one hundred
6 England France Italy Brazilian

8 Complete the conversations with these phrases.

> Can you repeat that, please?
> How do you say "mesa" in English?
> How do you spell 30?
> Open your books!
> ~~Please be quiet!~~
> What's the homework?

Please be quiet!

Learn the days of the week and months of the year for next class.

My birthday's in May.

Table.

T-h-i-r-t-y.

Grammar • To be

1 Complete the text with *'m, is/isn't, are/aren't*.

My name [1] *is* Natalia. I [2] .... twelve years old. I [3] .... from Colombia. This [4] .... Marco. He [5] .... Colombian. He [6] .... Italian. We [7] .... friends. We [8] .... in Italy or Colombia. We [9] .... in the United States on vacation.

2 Choose the correct options.

1 *I* / *You* 'm Australian.
2 *They* / *He* isn't at the park.
3 *We* / *She* are from Brazil.
4 *It* / *I* 's very tall.
5 *He* / *You* aren't fourteen.
6 *They* / *I* 'm not from London.

3 Look at the sentences in Exercise 2. Write opposite sentences.

1 *I'm not Australian.*
2 ....
3 ....
4 ....
5 ....
6 ....

4 Read the Visitors' Book. Write questions and answers about the nationalities.

• Visitors' Book •	
Name	**Country**
Bruce	England
Lucille	France
Luisa	Portugal
Nick and Theo	Greece
Javier	Spain
Rosa	Mexico
Mercedes	Mexico

1 Bruce / The US
  Is Bruce American?
  No, he isn't. He's English.
2 Lucille / France
  ....
  ....
3 Luisa / Brazil
  ....
  ....
4 Nick and Theo / Italy
  ....
  ....
5 Javier / Spain
  ....
  ....
6 Rosa and Mercedes / Mexico
  ....
  ....

• Wh questions

5 **Write and answer the questions.**

1 Why / here? / you / are
  Why are you here?
2 favorite / is / teacher? / Who / your
  ....
3 animal? / is / What / favorite / your
  ....
4 is / house? / your / Where
  ....
5 your / is / birthday? / When
  ....
6 old / How / you? / are
  ....

I'm here because this is my school.

....

....

....

....

....

• This/That/These/Those

6 **Complete the sentences with *This*, *That*, *These* or *Those*.**

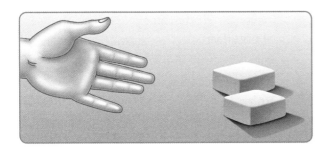

1 *These* are erasers.

2 .... is a calculator.

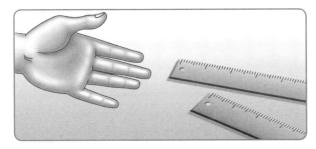

3 .... are rulers.

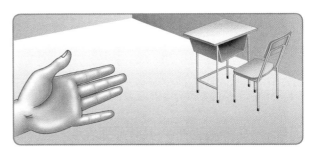

4 .... is a desk and a chair.

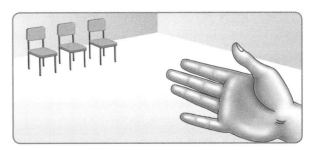

5 .... are chairs.

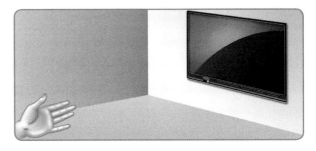

6 .... is an interactive whiteboard.

My World

Vocabulary • Objects

★ 1 **Find eight words in the word search. Match the words to the correct pictures (1-8).**

1   2   3   4

5   6   7   8

1 game console
2 ....
3 ....
4 ....
5 ....
6 ....
7 ....
8 ....

G	A	M	E	C	O	N	S	O	L	E	X
I	F	P	D	J	K	I	L	E	A	Z	M
G	B	3	U	M	B	D	L	Q	Z	W	A
A	M	P	W	T	H	V	V	I	W	A	G
T	P	L	F	P	C	D	W	I	A	T	A
S	K	A	T	E	B	O	A	R	D	C	Z
H	J	Y	C	I	N	A	D	I	S	H	I
I	C	E	S	K	A	T	E	S	T	S	N
Q	K	R	H	P	I	X	Q	G	Y	E	E
S	M	O	C	E	L	L	P	H	O	N	E

★ 2 **Put the letters in the correct order.**

1 occsmi   *comics*
2 otprse   ....
3 aletwl   ....
4 olptpa   ....
5 aecram   ....
6 igaurt   ....

★ 3 **Match the words in Exercise 2 to the pictures.**

a 6   b ☐   c ☐

d ☐   e ☐   f ☐

★★ 4 **Choose and write the word that doesn't belong.**

1 camera   chair   desk   table   *camera*
2 eleven   forty-three   cell phone
   twenty-five   ....
3 laptop   ice skates   game console
   MP3 player   ....
4 DVD   Spain   Italy   Mexico
   ....
5 pen   ruler   skateboard   eraser
   ....

★★ 5 **Choose a word from box A and a phrase from box B to complete the sentences.**

A	comic	~~guitar~~	laptop
	poster	skateboard	watch

B	a big picture	a board with wheels
	a computer	~~a musical instrument~~
	a small clock	a story with superheroes

1 A *guitar is a musical instrument.*
2 A .... is ....
3 A .... is ....
4 A .... is ....
5 A .... is ....
6 A .... is ....

Workbook page 116

Reading

★ (1) **Read the emails. Write Jon or Megan next to the objects.**

1 *Megan*

2 ....

3 ....

4 ....

5 ....

6 ....

★★ (2) **Read the emails again. Match the sentence beginnings (1–5) to the endings (a–e).**

1 *Connect Sports* is d
2 Jon is
3 Megan is
4 Miley Cyrus is
5 *Hannah Montana* is

a a fan of Miley Cyrus.
b a TV show about a teenage girl.
c a fan of computer games.
d a game for the computer.
e an actor in *Hannah Montana*.

★★ (3) **Read and write true (T), false (F) or don't know (DK).**

1 Jon is a soccer fan.   DK
2 He's happy because it's his birthday.   ....
3 The game is from his brother.   ....
4 The Miley Cyrus concert is today.   ....
5 Hannah Montana is a pop star at night. ....
6 The photos of Miley are on the table.   ....

★★ (4) **Answer the questions.**

1 Is the watch from Jon's grandma? *Yes, it is.*
2 Is the book from his friend? ....
3 How many sports are on *Connect Sports*?
   ....
4 Does Megan have a ticket for a Miley Cyrus concert? ....
5 Are the photos of Miley Cyrus from magazines? ....

New Message   ⊗

Send

Hi Megan,

How are you? I'm really happy because it's my birthday today. I got a watch from my grandma, a book from my brother and a wallet from my friend, Liam. The watch is blue, and the wallet's brown. My favorite present is from my mom and dad. It's a computer game, *Connect Sports*. It's amazing. It has soccer and volleyball, and four other sports. All my family are fans of the game. It's time to go because my friends are here, and my party is about to begin.

Jon

New Message   ⊗

Send

Hi Jon,

Happy Birthday! Today's a good day for me too because I have a ticket for a Miley Cyrus concert tonight. I'm a Miley Cyrus fan. Miley is the star of *Hannah Montana*, a TV show about a girl who goes to school during the day but is a pop star at night. I have Hannah Montana DVDs and a lot of songs on my MP3 player. On my bedroom walls, I have posters and photos of Miley from magazines. It's five o'clock now and the concert is at seven. Time to get ready!

Megan

Grammar • Have

★ 1 Choose the correct options.

1 We *have* / *has* our skateboards for the park.
2 He *don't have* / *doesn't have* a poster of the Cowboys football team on the wall.
3 My parents *have* / *has* a big car.
4 She *have* / *has* an autograph book with a lot of famous names in it.
5 I *don't have* / *doesn't have* my cell phone with me.

★ 2 Complete the questions and answers with *do/don't* or *does/doesn't*.

1 Do you have your camera?   Yes, I *do*.
2 .... you and Wendy have your ice skates?   Yes, we do.
3 .... she have her lunch? No, she doesn't.
4 Do Ed and Paul have a game console? No, they ....
5 Does your dad have his laptop with him? Yes, he ....

★★ 3 Look at the pictures and complete the sentences. Use the correct form of *have*.

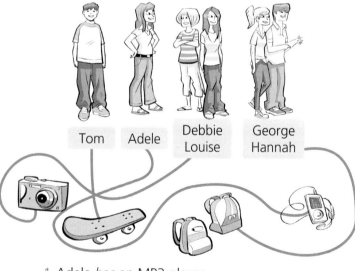

Tom   Adele   Debbie Louise   George Hannah

1 Adele *has* an MP3 player.
2 Debbie and Louise .... a skateboard.
3 Tom .... a camera.
4 George and Hannah .... backpacks.
5 Tom .... a skateboard.
6 Debbie and Louise .... a camera.

★★ 4 Look at the list and write Mohammed's sentences.

In my backpack
magazine ✓
pens ✗
cell phone ✓
wallet ✓
guitar ✗

1 I have my magazine.

2 I .... pens.

3 I .... cell phone.

4 I .... wallet.

5 I .... guitar.

★★ 5 Write questions. Then look at the pictures and answer the questions.

1 he / a guitar
Does he have a guitar?   Yes, he does.
2 they / laptops
....
....
3 she / a watch
....
....
4 it / a ball
....
....
5 he / a cell phone
....
....
6 they / skateboards
....
....

Grammar Reference pages 108–109

Vocabulary • Adjectives

★ 1 Read and choose the correct options.

1 It's my birthday today. I have a new bike.

a ☐   b ☑

2 This show is very interesting.

a ☐   b ☐

3 This puzzle isn't difficult. It's really easy.

a ☐   b ☐

4 A I have that cell phone. It's very cheap.
  B Yes, it isn't expensive. It's great.

a ☐   b ☐

5 I don't have a big family, so we have a small car.

a ☐   b ☐

Brain Trainer

**Learn opposite adjectives in pairs.
Now do Exercise 2.**

★ 2 Write the opposite adjectives. Use these words.

bad	boring	cheap
easy	~~old~~	unpopular

1 new   *old*
2 interesting ....
3 popular   ....
4 difficult   ....
5 good   ....
6 expensive   ....

★★ 3 Complete the sentences with these words.

~~boring~~	difficult	expensive
good	new	popular

1 This book isn't interesting. It's *boring*.
2 That hotel isn't cheap. It's really ....
3 I have a lot of homework today, and it's
   ....
4 My dad has an old laptop, but mom's laptop is
   ....
5 Mr. Brown's a very unpopular teacher,
   but Ms. Scarlett is ....
6 It isn't a bad movie. It's ....

★★ 4 Choose the correct options.

My dad has a ¹(new)/ *easy* cell
phone. A lot of people have
the same cell. It's ² *popular /
old* because it's very ³ *bad /
good*. It's also ⁴ *small / boring*
and really ⁵ *easy / unpopular*
to use. He's happy. My mom
isn't happy because it's very
⁶ *interesting / expensive*.

★★ 5 Complete the sentences with your own ideas.

1 *Cell phones* are expensive.
2 .... is a good movie.
3 .... is a popular singer.
4 .... is a boring TV show.
5 .... is a big country.
6 .... are old.
7 .... is a difficult subject.
8 .... are small animals.

Workbook page 116

Chatroom Talking about position

Speaking and Listening

★ **1** Listen and read the conversation.
3   Underline the prepositions of place.

> **Frank** This is my classroom. We have a new interactive whiteboard.
> **Beth** Great. Where's your desk?
> **Frank** It's <u>behind</u> Laura's. Her desk is in front of my desk.
> **Beth** Is it the desk next to the window?
> **Frank** Yes, it has a ruler on it, and my backpack is under the chair.
> **Beth** You have a lot in your backpack. What's in it?
> **Frank** Pens, pencils, books and my cleats.
> **Beth** Why do you have cleats in your backpack?
> **Frank** They're my soccer cleats. I have a soccer game now. Let's go.
> **Beth** OK.

★ **2** Read the conversation again. Answer the questions.

1 Where are Frank and Beth?
They're in the classroom.
2 Where's Frank's desk?
....
3 Where's Laura's desk?
....
4 Where's the ruler?
....
5 Where's Frank's backpack?
....
6 Where are Frank's soccer cleats?
....

★★ **3** Look at the picture. Complete the sentences with these words.

| behind | in | in front of | next to | on | under |

1 The table is *behind the guitar.*
2 The comics are ....
3 The skateboard is ....
4 The ice skates are ....
5 The backpack is ....
6 The boy is ....

★★ **4** Listen and choose the correct options.
4

> **Frank** Mom, where's my cell phone?
> **Mom** Is it ¹ (on) / under the table?
> **Frank** No, it isn't. And it isn't ² behind / next to the TV.
> **Mom** Is it ³ in / under your bed?
> **Frank** No, it isn't there.
> **Mom** Where's your backpack?
> **Frank** It's ⁴ behind / on the door.
> **Mom** Is it ⁵ in / next to your backpack?
> **Frank** Oh yes. Here it is. Thanks, Mom.

★★ **5** Read the conversation again. Where's Frank's cell phone?

★★ **6** Think of an object in your bedroom. Write a conversation between you and your mom about where it is. Use the model in Exercise 4.

Speaking and Listening page 120

Grammar • Possessive adjectives and Possessive 's

★ 1 Rewrite the sentences with the apostrophes in the correct place.

1 Here is the cats dinner.
   Here is the cat's dinner.
2 Do you have Johns magazines?
   ....
3 That is my parents laptop.
   ....
4 Those are Amandas DVDs.
   ....
5 When is Bens moms birthday?
   ....

> **Brain Trainer**
>
> **With a new grammar point, memorize the new words or structures as a group.**
>
> Write the possessive adjectives for each pronoun.
>
> | I | *my* | it | .... |
> |---|------|-----|-----|
> | you | .... | we | .... |
> | he | .... | they | .... |
> | she | .... | | |
>
> **Now do Exercise 2.**

★ 2 Choose the correct options.

1 It's a friendly dog. (His) / *Their* name is Sunny.
2 You have an English class now. Do you have *its / your* books?
3 My brother and I have basketball posters. *Our / Your* favorite team is the Knicks.
4 She doesn't have an expensive cell phone. *Her / My* phone is cheap.
5 They're tall children. *Their / Your* parents are tall.
6 I have a big bedroom. *His / My* bed is next to the window.

★ 3 Complete the sentences.

1 It's *Ella's* (Ella) bag.
2 They're .... (Charlie) books.
3 This is .... (Jenny and Ed) dog.
4 She has .... (her mom) camera.
5 Is it .... (your parents) car?

★★ 4 Complete the conversation with these words.

her	his	its	~~my~~	our	their	your

Ed Hello. I'm Ed.
Jo Hi, Ed. [1] *My* name's Jo. Are you here with [2] .... family?
Ed No, I'm not. This is my friend Susie and [3] .... brother. [4] .... name is Adam.
Jo Do they have a dog? Is that [5] .... dog in that bag?
Ed No, it isn't, but we have [6] .... picnic lunch in that bag!
Jo Look! Is that [7] .... ball?
Ed Yes, it is. Let's throw it.
Jo Get the ball! Good dog.
Ed Thanks, Jo.

★★ 5 Look at the pictures and write sentences.

1 autograph book
   It's Jane's autograph book.
2 backpacks
   ....
   ....

3 bedroom
   ....
   ....
4 notebooks
   ....
   ....

Grammar Reference pages 108–109

Reading

1 Read the text quickly. Match the photos to the descriptions.

 a  b 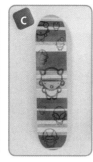 c  d

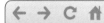

1 Photo *c*

This awesome red-and-white skateboard is new. It's 75 cm long, and it has black wheels. It's for children over ten years old, and it has a DVD with skateboarding lessons. Now only $35.

2 Photo .....

For all Justin Bieber fans, here are some special items for your collection: a Justin Bieber poster for your wall, his *My World* and *Under the Mistletoe* CDs, and a really cool photo of Justin with his autograph! All for $60.

3 Photo .....

Here is a great collection of 20 comics from 2008 to 2011, including many of the popular *Fantastic Four* and *Commando* comics. They're really good, and they have a lot of exciting stories and pictures. Buy them all for $8.

4 Photo .....

This small blue guitar is in very good condition. It has a black bag, a music book and a DVD. This guitar is expensive when new, but here it's only $37.

2 Read the descriptions again. Write the correct object below the sentences.

1 It has his autograph on it.
Justin Bieber photo
2 It's thirty-seven dollars.
....
3 It has a DVD with skateboarding lessons.
....
4 It has a music book with it.
....
5 They're eight dollars.
....

3 Read the descriptions again. Answer the questions.

1 Is the skateboard old? *No, it isn't.*
2 Is the poster of Justin Bieber?
....
3 Are the DVDs for Justin Bieber fans?
....
4 Are the comics new?
....
5 Are the *Commando* comics popular?
....
6 Is the guitar big?
....
7 Does the guitar have a blue bag?
....

Listening

1 Listen and choose the correct option.
5
Who is Kim's favorite actor?
a Zac Efron
b Leonardo DiCaprio
c Daniel Radcliffe

2 Listen again. Choose the correct options.
5
1 Kim has a new poster / camera.
2 She has *two / three* High School Musical DVDs.
3 Zac's in *Hairspray / The Karate Kid*.
4 Kim has Zac's songs on her *laptop / MP3 player*.
5 Zac is a *singer and dancer / DJ*.

3 Listen again. Answer the questions.
5
1 Is the poster in a bag?
Yes, it is.
2 Is the poster for Kim's bedroom?
....
3 Are the *High School Musical* movies popular?
....
4 Does Kim have the *17 Again* DVD?
....
5 Do the *High School Musical* movies have a lot of songs in them?
....

Writing • A personal profile

1 **Rewrite the sentences. Use capital letters, periods and apostrophes.**

1 its a nice bedroom
   It's a nice bedroom.
2 helens room has pink walls
....
3 her rooms window is small
....
4 shes a selena gomez fan
....
5 she doesnt have a lot of magazines
....
6 helens family is in the photo
....

2 **Read the description of Helen's bedroom and find the false sentence in Exercise 1.**

My bedroom
My room is very nice. It has a small window and yellow walls. I have a table next to my bed, a closet with all my clothes, a desk and a chair.
All my favorite things are in my bedroom. I'm a big Selena Gomez fan, and I have a poster of her on my wall. My collection of magazines and my MP3 player are on my desk. I also have a photo of my family on the table next to my bed.

3 **Read the description again. Look at the table and write sentences.**

The table			the closet.
Her clothes		in	the bed.
The poster	is	on	the wall.
Her MP3 player	are	next to	the desk.
The photo			the table.

1 *The table is next to the bed.*
2 ....
3 ....
4 ....
5 ....

4 **Think about your bedroom. Answer the questions.**

1 What color is your bedroom?
....
2 Is your room big or small?
....
3 What furniture (bed, table, etc.) is in your room?
....
4 What is on the walls?
....
5 What objects do you have in your room?
....

5 **Write two paragraphs about your bedroom. Use the model in Exercise 2 and the information in Exercise 4.**

Paragraph 1
Describe your bedroom and the furniture.

Paragraph 2
Write what is in your room.

My room is ....
....
....
....
....
....
....
....
....
....
....

2 Around Town

Vocabulary • Places in a town

★ **1** Complete the puzzle. Find the hidden place.

1	b	a	n	k

★ **2** Match the words to make four places. Then look at the picture in Exercise 1 and write the correct number.

1 town ⟍   a station ☐
2 post   ⟍   b square ☐
3 bus   c complex ☐
4 sports   d office ☐

★★ **3** Look at the picture in Exercise 1. Complete the sentences with these words.

bank	~~police station~~	movie theater
hospital	library	train station

1 The town square is behind the *police station*.
2 The post office is next to the ....
3 The park is in front of the ....
4 The sports complex is behind the ....
5 The museum is next to the ....
6 The café is next to the ....

★★ **4** Put the words in the correct order.

1 square / in / it's / town / No, / the
  No, it's in the town square.
2 me, / is / bank / here / Excuse / the / near / ?
  ....
3 hospital / it / the / Is / behind / ?
  ....
4 much / you / Thank / very
  ....
5 the / next / it's / office / Yes, / post / to
  ....

★★ **5** Number the sentences from Exercise 4 in the correct order.

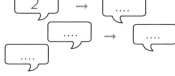

Paul   2 → ....
        .... → ....
        ....   Jen

Workbook page 117

Reading

★ **1** **Read the postcard. Mark the places in Hull.**

1 bank	☐	7 museum	☐
2 movie theater	☐	8 restaurant	☐
3 library	☐	9 post office	☐
4 sports complex	☐	10 park	☐
5 town square	☐	11 shopping mall	☐
6 supermarket	☐	12 café	☐

★ **2** **Read the postcard again. Write the correct places.**

> the banks   the café   the hotel
> the park   ~~the supermarket~~

1 It's in the town square.   *the supermarket*
2 It's next to the post office.   ....
3 They are in the town square.   ....
4 It's in front of the hotel.   ....
5 It's behind the hotel.   ....

★ **3** **Are the statements true (T) or false (F)?**

1 Hull is next to the ocean.   *T*
2 Hull doesn't have a beach.   ....
3 Hull has a shopping mall.   ....
4 The town has an Italian restaurant
   in the town square.   ....
5 There are a lot of seagulls in Hull.   ....
6 The café has delicious pizzas.   ....

★★ **4** **Answer the questions.**

1 Is Josh in Hull with his family?
   Yes, he is.
2 Is it hot and sunny in Hull?
   ....
3 Is Hull a small town?
   ....
4 Is the beach behind the hotel?
   ....
5 Is the hotel next to a bank?
   ....
6 Is the ice cream good?
   ....

Hi Chris,
How are you? I'm in Hull with my family. Hull is a seaside town with a great beach.
We're here on vacation, but the weather is terrible. There isn't much to do here when
the weather's bad. It's a small town. There aren't any museums or movie theaters.
There isn't a library, a sports complex or a shopping mall. There are some stores
in the town square. There's also a supermarket, two banks, an Italian restaurant
(they have delicious pizzas) and two post offices. Our hotel is next to a post office.
Behind the hotel, there are a few houses, a park and then the beach. There are a lot
of seagulls in this town!
In front of the hotel, there's a very good café. We have lunch there every day.
The chocolate ice cream is great. How is your vacation?
See you next week.
Love from Josh

Grammar • There is/There are; Some/Any

★ **(1)** **Read the text. Mark the places in the town.**

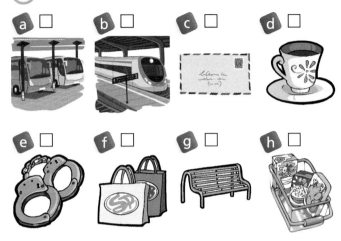

a ☐   b ☐   c ☐   d ☐

e ☐   f ☐   g ☐   h ☐

In my town, there's a bus station, but there isn't a train station. There are two cafés, but there aren't any restaurants. My favorite café is next to the post office. There isn't a supermarket, but there are some small stores. There's a police station. My house is in the center of town. It's next to a beautiful park.

★ **(2)** **Choose the correct options.**

1 *There's* / *There are* a bus station in the town.
2 **A** *Is there* / *Are there* a café at the train station?
  B No, *there aren't* / *there isn't*.
3 Are there *any* / *some* old stores in the town square?
4 There are *any* / *some* big trees in the park.

★★ **(3)** **Complete the sentences with *There is/There are* (✓) or *There isn't/There aren't* (✗).**

1 *There is* a new TV show about sports. ✓
2 .... any comics in my backpack. ✗
3 .... a cell phone on the table. ✗
4 .... some magazines under my bed. ✓
5 .... a camera in my backpack. ✓
6 .... any posters on the walls. ✗

★★ **(4)** **Look at the picture. Make sentences with these words.**

	some pretty	tree
	a small	flowers
There's	three	dog
There are	a big	bikes
	two	people
	one	guitar

1 *There are some pretty flowers.*
2 ....
3 ....
4 ....
5 ....
6 ....

★★ **(5)** **Write the questions. Then look at the picture in Exercise 4 and answer.**

1 any birds?
  Are there any birds?
  Yes, there are.
2 a cat?
  ....
  ....
3 any magazines?
  ....
  ....
4 a swimming pool?
  ....
  ....
5 any lawn chairs?
  ....
  ....
6 a house?
  ....
  ....

Grammar Reference pages 110–111

Vocabulary • Action verbs

★ **(1)** **Put the letters in the correct order. Then mark the correct pictures.**

1 wsmi   *swim*
2 gjuleg   ....
3 adcne   ....
4 tsaek   ....
5 bcilm   ....
6 eibk   ....

1 **a** ☑   **b** ☐

2 **a** ☐   **b** ☐

3 **a** ☐   **b** ☐

4 **a** ☐   **b** ☐

5 **a** ☐   **b** ☐

6 **a** ☐   **b** ☐

★ **(2)** **Match the activities to the pictures you didn't mark in Exercise 1.**

| fly | jump | play | ~~run~~ | sing | walk |

1 *run*   4 ....
2 .... 5 ....
3 .... 6 ....

★★ **(3)** **Find and write the activities.**

lunch (skate) park cat bike
walk fish eraser cheap juggle
camera swim sing comics hospital

1 *skate*   4 ....
2 .... 5 ....
3 .... 6 ....

> **Brain Trainer**
>
> English spelling can be difficult. Learn the pronunciation <u>and</u> the spelling of each new word. Do you say these words as you write them?
> *walk   talk   climb*
>
> **Now do Exercise 4.**

★★ **(4)** **Circle the words with a silent letter and write the letter. Then listen and check.**
6

(walk)   *l*   guitar   ....
bike   ....   talk   ....
climb   ....   know   ....
skate   ....   dance   ....

★★★ **(5)** **Complete the phrases with these words. Then add your own ideas.**

| the guitar | a kite | a race |
| six oranges | ~~a song~~ | a tree |

1 sing *a song, the words*
2 fly .... , ...
3 run .... , ...
4 climb .... , ...
5 juggle .... , ...
6 play .... , ...

Workbook page 117

Chatroom Orders and warnings

Speaking and Listening

★ **1** **Match the words and phrases.**

1 Be   a shout!
2 Please   b me!
3 Don't   c for us!
4 Wait   d in the street.
5 Watch   e careful!
6 Don't play   f don't do that!

★ **2** **Read and listen to the conversation. <u>Underline</u>**
7 **and write the orders and warnings.**

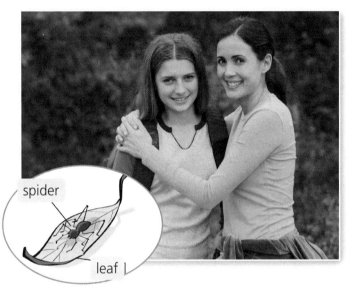

spider

leaf

Mom	It's a beautiful day. We can walk to the lake and have lunch there. There's a café next to the lake.
Beth	Mom, there's a spider on your head!
Mom	Oh no! <u>Help!</u>
Beth	Don't shout! Don't touch it!
Mom	Please help me. I don't like spiders.
Beth	Don't move! Be quiet!
Mom	Come on, Beth. Where is it?
Beth	I don't know. I can't see it now.
Mom	But what's this? This isn't a spider. It's a leaf!
Beth	Sorry, Mom. You're right. It's only a leaf.

1 *Help!*
2 ....
3 ....
4 ....
5 ....

★★ **3** **Complete the conversation with these phrases.**
8 **Then listen and check.**

~~Come here, Mom.~~	Don't play with it!
Don't shout!	Don't stand in front of it.
Look!	

Beth	¹ *Come here, Mom.*
Mom	What is it, Beth?
Beth	² .... There's a hedgehog!
Mom	Shh! ³ .... It's asleep!
Beth	It isn't asleep now.
Mom	⁴ .... It isn't a pet.
Beth	It can walk very quickly!
Mom	Yes, it can. ⁵ .... It wants to go that way.
Beth	It's in the tall grass now. That's a really good place for it.
Mom	Yes, it is.

★★★ **4** **Look at the picture and write a conversation between you and a friend. Use the conversation in Exercise 3 as your model. Use your own ideas, or the warnings below.**

Be quiet!
Be careful!
Don't touch it.
Don't go near it.
Don't move.

....
....
....
....

Speaking and Listening page 121

Grammar • *Can/Can't* for ability

★ **(1)** Complete the sentences with *can* or *can't* and one of these verbs.

| climb | fly | ~~jump~~ | skateboard | walk |

1 The dog *can jump* very high.
2 The boy ....
3 The cat .... a tree.
4 The girl .... a kite.
5 The baby ....

★ **(2)** Complete the answers.

1 **A** Can you skate?
  B No, *I can't.*
2 **A** Can you run a kilometer?
  B Yes, ...
3 **A** Can your dog swim?
  B Yes, ...
4 **A** Can they dance well?
  B No, ...
5 **A** Can your dad juggle?
  B No, ...
6 **A** Can she climb that mountain?
  B Yes, ...

★★ **(3)** What can Laura do? Complete the sentences.

 ✓
1
Laura *can* play the guitar.

 ✗
2
She .... sing opera.

 ✓
3
.... ride a bike.

 ✗
4
.... skate.

 ✗
5
.... juggle four balls.

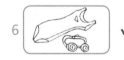 ✓
6
.... swim.

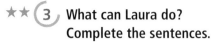

★★ **(4)** Put the words in the correct order to make questions. Then answer the questions.

1 you / Can / 100 meters? / run
  Can you run 100 meters?
  Yes, I can. / No, I can't.
2 the / your / play / dad / guitar? / Can
  ....
  ....
3 Can / dance? / your / sing / mom / and
  ....
  ....
4 your / skate? / you / and / Can / friends
  ....
  ....
5 mountain? / you / a / a / or / tree / Can / climb
  ....
  ....

Grammar Reference pages 110–111

Reading

1 Read the text quickly. Mark the correct picture.

1 ☐ 2 ☐ 3 ☐

18

Sasha and Alex are at the train station. It's late, and there are some bad men in the train station, too. They can see the men in front of a café, but the men can't see them.

Sasha and Alex can't go to a hotel because they don't have any money, but Alex has an idea. His aunt has a house in the town. The house is next to a toy museum. There's a map of the town on the wall next to the ticket office. They can find the directions and walk to his aunt's house.

It's a big town. There are a lot of streets and houses. There are also two or three shopping malls and a large park. There's a sports complex in the park. Sasha and Alex can find the police station, the bus station, the town square and some schools on the map, but they can't find the museum. Suddenly, Sasha sees it. At the same moment, they can hear one of the men behind them. They run.

2 Read the text again. Match the sentence beginnings (1–5) to the endings (a–e).

1 Sasha and Alex are at the *d*
2 The men are in front of a
3 The map is next to the
4 Alex's aunt's house is next to the
5 There's a sports complex in the

a museum.
b ticket office.
c park.
d train station.
e café.

3 Answer the questions.

1 Is it early in the morning? *No, it isn't. It's late.*
2 Can Sasha and Alex see the bad men?

....

3 Can they go to Alex's aunt's house?

....

4 Are there any mountains on the map?

....

5 Is there a police station on the map?

....

Listening

Brain Trainer

Don't worry if you don't understand everything you hear. Guess what the person says.

Now do Exercise 1.

1 Listen to Tom and Maddy. Mark the places you hear.

9

1 movie theater ☐   5 bank ☐
2 library ☐   6 park ☐
3 police station ☐   7 train station ☐
4 museum ☐

2 Listen again. Choose the correct options.

9

1 Maddy has the (*map*) / *camera*.
2 They're next to a *bus station* / *police station*.
3 The statue's in front of a *museum* / *park*.
4 Maddy can see a *library* / *train station*.
5 The movie theater's *on the next street* / *in the shopping mall*.

3 Answer the questions.

1 Is Maddy tired? *Yes, she is.*
2 Does Tom have the map?

....

3 Does Maddy have a camera in her backpack?

....

4 Is there a statue of a horse?

....

5 Where are Tom and Maddy?

....

6 Does Tom have the movie tickets?

....

Writing • A description of a town

1 **Complete the sentences with *and*, *or*, *but*.**

1 There's a café *and* two restaurants in the town.
2 There isn't a sports complex ....
   a swimming pool near my house.
3 She can't sing, ... she can dance
   really well.
4 There are a lot of small stores, ...
   there isn't a supermarket.
5 You can swim in a swimming pool
   .... the ocean.
6 I can juggle, ... I can ride a unicycle.

2 **Complete the text with these words.**

| afternoon | and | ~~bike~~ | can | interesting |
| mall | or | station | theater | |

A day trip to Stratford
In the morning, we can ¹ *bike* to the town square.
There's a big shopping ² .... next
to the police ³ .... It has a lot
of cool stores.
In the ⁴ .... , we can visit the museum.
It's expensive, but it's very ⁵ .... There
are statues, posters, old books ⁶ ....
some beautiful paintings. There's a wonderful
painting of some people in a café. It's my favorite.
In the evening, we ⁷ .... go to an
Italian restaurant, ⁸ .... we can watch
a movie at the movie ⁹ ....

3 **Read the description in Exercise 2 and write
the places.**

1 *town square*   5 ....
2 ....   6 ....
3 ....   7 ....
4 ....   8 ....

4 **Look at the brochure. Mark the things you can
do in Charlton.**

☐ go shopping
☐ skateboard in the park
☐ visit the museum
☐ watch a movie at the theater
☐ play sports
☐ swim in the pool
☐ have lunch in a Chinese restaurant
☐ have dinner in a French restaurant

5 **Now write a description of Charlton. Use the
model in Exercise 2 and the ideas in Exercise 4.**

A day trip to Charlton
In the morning, we can ....
....
....
In the afternoon, ...
....
....
In the evening, ...
....
....

3 School Days

Vocabulary • Daily routines

Brain Trainer

Learn words that go together:
get dressed   have breakfast   watch TV

Now do Exercise 1.

★ **1** **Match the words to make daily routines.**

1 I meet   a my homework.
2 We start   b my friends.
3 I clean up   c my teeth.
4 We have   d my room.
5 I brush   e lunch.
6 I do   f school.

★ **2** **Look at the pictures. Complete the sentences with these phrases.**

> get dressed   ~~get up~~   go home   go to bed
> have breakfast   have dinner   take a shower

Bill

1 I *get up.*
2 I ....
3 I ....
4 I ....

Sam

5 I ....
6 I ....
7 I ....

★★ **3** **Look at Exercise 2. Read the sentences and choose the correct name.**

1 I get up early.   *Sam / Bill*
2 I have dinner with my family.   *Sam / Bill*
3 I take a shower in the morning.   *Sam / Bill*
4 I go to bed at 10 p.m.   *Sam / Bill*
5 I have breakfast with my sister.   *Sam / Bill*

★★ **4** **Write these words under the correct verb.**

> dressed   ~~home~~   lunch
> to school   breakfast   up

go	have	get
home	....	....
....	....	....

★★ **5** **Complete the text with *go, take, have* or *get*.**

Every morning, I [1] *get* up early. I [2] ....
a shower, and then I [3] .... dressed.
I [4] .... breakfast with my family,
and then I [5] .... to school.
We start school at 9 o'clock. At 1 o'clock,
we [6] .... lunch. After school,
I [7] .... home and do my
homework. I [8] .... dinner and
watch TV in the evening. I [9] ....
to bed at 10 o'clock.

> **Workbook** page 118

Reading 🎧

★ **1** Read the magazine article. Mark the activities Antonio does.

1 ☐

2 ☐

3 ☐

4 ☐

5 ☐

6  ☐

★ **2** Read the article again. Match the sentence beginnings (1–6) to the endings (a–f).

1 Antonio has
2 His sister is
3 Antonio can
4 His mom is
5 His tennis lessons are
6 The family has

a four years old.
b a tennis coach.
c a small family.
d at the gym.
e dinner together.
f play tennis.

★★ **3** Choose the correct options.

1 Antonio *has* / *doesn't have* a big family.
2 His family *likes* / *doesn't like* tennis.
3 He *goes* / *doesn't go* to the gym with his sister.
4 Antonio's stepdad *is* / *isn't* his tennis coach.
5 He *goes* / *doesn't go* home after his tennis lesson.
6 He *goes* / *doesn't go* to bed early.

★★★ **4** Read the article again. Answer the questions.

1 How many people are there in Antonio's family?
There are four people.
2 Can Antonio's sister play tennis?
....
3 Is Antonio's tennis practice before breakfast?
....
4 Is Antonio's tennis lesson after school?
....
5 Does he have a computer in his bedroom?
....
6 Is Antonio tired in the evening?
....

A Day in the Life of
… the Tennis Star, **Antonio Perez!**

I have a small family. There's my mom, my stepdad, my sister and me. We all love tennis—my sister can play tennis, and she's only four years old!

On school days, I get up at 5:30 a.m. and get dressed in my tennis clothes. I have breakfast, and then my mom and I go to the gym together. She works there. I play tennis for an hour before school. After tennis, I take a shower and get dressed in my school uniform. I meet my friends at 8:20 a.m., and we walk to school together. School starts at 9 a.m.

After school, I go to the gym again. I have a tennis lesson at 4:15 p.m. with my mom. She's my tennis coach. Then we go home. My stepdad doesn't get home until 6 p.m. We have dinner together at 6:30 p.m., and then I do my homework. From 7 to 8 p.m., I watch TV or play computer games in my bedroom. I go to bed early because I'm tired—I get up very early in the morning.

Grammar • Present simple: affirmative and negative

★ **1** Complete the sentences with these verbs. Use each verb twice.

> do ~~go~~ go have play watch

1 I *go* home after school, but my brother *goes* to the park.
2 I .... on the computer, but my brother .... soccer.
3 I .... eggs for dinner, but my brother .... pizza.
4 I .... my homework in my bedroom, but my brother .... his homework in the living room.
5 I .... old movies on TV, but my brother .... sports.
6 I .... to bed at 9 p.m., but my brother .... to bed at 9:30 p.m.

★ **2** Complete the sentences with *don't/doesn't* and the correct form of the verbs.

1 My friends and I go to the town square on the weekend. We *don't go* to the park.
2 I get up early on school days.
   I .... early on the weekend.
3 My dad takes a shower in the morning.
   He .... a shower in the evening.
4 My sister reads magazines.
   She .... books.
5 Sunita and Raoul play soccer.
   They .... basketball.
6 Our dog likes my friends.
   He .... the mail carrier.

★★ **3** Choose the correct *-s* ending for these verbs. Then listen and check.
10

1 looks   ⟨/s/⟩   /z/   /ɪz/
2 goes   /s/   /z/   /ɪz/
3 dances   /s/   /z/   /ɪz/
4 swims   /s/   /z/   /ɪz/
5 meets   /s/   /z/   /ɪz/
6 watches   /s/   /z/   /ɪz/

★★ **4** Complete the description with the Present simple form of the verbs.

Every Saturday morning, I [1] *clean up* (clean up) my room. Lydia, my sister, [2] .... (clean up) her room too, but my room is more messy! Then I [3] .... (clean) out the rabbits' hutches, and Lydia [4] .... (give) the fish some food. After lunch, we [5] .... (go) to the park together. My sister [6] .... (bike), but I [7] .... (walk) because I don't have a bike. We sometimes [8] .... (meet) our friends and [9] .... (play) soccer. In the evening, we [10] .... (not go) out. We [11] .... (watch) TV. I [12] .... (like) game shows, but Lydia [13] .... (not like) them. She [14] .... (like) *The X Factor* and *The Voice*.

★★ **5** Write sentences about the pictures. Use the Present simple affirmative and negative.

1 bike to school / walk
   The students *don't bike to school. They walk.*
2 watch TV / read books
   The girl ....
3 go to the park / play computer games at home
   The boy ....
4 go to the movies / have a picnic
   The friends ....
5 study French / study English
   He ....
6 play soccer / do a puzzle
   I ....

> **Grammar Reference** pages 112–113

Vocabulary • School subjects

★ 1 **Read the texts and number the subjects.**

a music ☐   d computer science ☐
b math ☐   e French ☐
c PE ☐   f English ☐1

1 **Teacher**   Good morning, everyone. Open your books to page 27. Today, we are learning the words for school subjects.
2 **Teacher**   Simon, what is 128 plus 6 plus 25?
   Boy   159.
   Teacher   That's right.
3 **Teacher**   Today, we are listening to Beethoven.
4 **Teacher**   Today, we are looking at different computer programs.
5 **Teacher**   Get ready. Go!
6 **Girl**   Bonjour, Madame. Comment allez-vous?
   Teacher   Très bien, merci.

★ 2 **Complete the crossword with these words.**

art   English   geography   history
computer science   literature   math   science

Across

Down

★★ 3 **Match the sentence beginnings (1–6) to the subjects (a–f).**

1 We write essays about society in *e*
2 We run and play games in
3 We learn grammar, listen to CDs and talk in pairs in
4 We read about different countries in
5 We learn about computers and how to use them in
6 We work with numbers in

a English.
b math.
c PE.
d computer science.
e social studies.
f geography.

★★ 4 **Write the classes.**

art   French   literature   music   ~~PE~~   science

1 We play soccer in the winter and tennis in the summer.   *PE*
2 Our teacher plays the piano and we sing. ....
3 We read a lot of books. My favorite book is *To Kill a Mockingbird.* ....
4 Our teacher explains the grammar, and we speak in pairs. ....
5 We look at famous paintings, and then we draw or paint pictures. ....
6 We learn about the body and plants. ....

★★ 5 **Complete the sentences to make them true.**

1 I have .... and .... on Wednesday.
2 .... is my geography teacher.
3 I play .... in PE.
4 My science classes are on .... and ....
5 I write essays in ....
6 My favorite subject is ....

Workbook page 118

Speaking and Listening

★ **1** Listen and read the conversation. <u>Underline</u>
11 phrases for asking and answering about time.

Frank	Let's do our English homework together.
Beth	OK.
Frank	<u>What time is it?</u>
Beth	It's one thirty.
Frank	School gets out at three ten. Can you come to my house at three thirty?
Beth	I can't today because I have a piano lesson.
Frank	What time does your lesson start?
Beth	It's at a quarter to four.
Frank	And what time does it end?
Beth	It's half an hour. It ends at four fifteen.
Frank	Can you come to my house after that?
Beth	Yes, that's fine. I can be there at four forty.
Frank	Good. You can have dinner at my house, and my mom can drive you home at eight o'clock.
Beth	OK. Thanks. See you later.

★ **2** Read the conversation again. Match the times to the activities.

1.   a go home

2.   b piano lesson ends

3.   c school gets out

4.   d piano lesson starts

5.   e go to Frank's house

★★ **3** Look at the clocks. Write the times.

1   2   3   4   5

1 *It's twenty past two.   It's two twenty.*
2 ....
3 ....
4 ....
5 ....

★★ **4** Put the conversation in order.

a ☐ When does it end?
b ☑ What time is it?
c ☐ What time does it start?
d ☐ OK. Let's watch that.
e ☐ It's twenty past six. What's on TV tonight?
f ☐ It starts at seven o'clock.
g ☐ There's a great monster movie.
h ☐ At eight forty.

★★ **5** Write the conversation from Exercise 4 in order.
12 Then listen and check.

1 *What time is it?*
2 ....
3 ....
4 ....
5 ....
6 ....
7 ....
8 ....

★★ **6** You want to watch TV today. Choose a show from the TV schedule below and write a conversation between you and a friend. Use the model in Exercise 5.

7:30	**The Simpsons**
7:45	**Movie: The Great Chicken Race**
9:15	**A History of Clocks**
9:45	**The Funny Ha Ha Show**
10:10	**The Sports Quiz**

Speaking and Listening page 122

Grammar • Present simple: questions and short answers

★ 1 Complete the questions with *Do* or *Does*.

1 *Do* you know any movie stars?
2 .... she like ice cream?
3 .... they go to the movies every week?
4 .... the movie start at 7:30?
5 .... you and your family play a lot of sports?
6 ....your dad watch TV in the evening?

★ 2 Match the questions to the answers. Then choose the correct verb.

1 Do you and your family get up early?   *d*
2 Do you brush your teeth after breakfast?
3 Does your dad take a shower in the morning?
4 Does your room usually look neat?
5 Does your sister walk to school?
6 Do your mom and dad work together?

a No, they *don't / doesn't*.
b Yes, it *do / does*.
c Yes, she *do / does*.
d No, we *don't / doesn't*.
e Yes, I *do / does*.
f No, he *don't / doesn't*.

★ 3 Complete the questions with *Do* or *Does*. Then answer the questions.

1 *Do* you go to school by bus?
   Yes, I do. / No, I don't.
2 .... you and your friends study French at school?   ....
3 .... your English teacher use an interactive whiteboard?   ....
4 .... your friends have lunch at school?
   ....
5 .... your best friend like art?
   ....

★★ 4 Look at the chart and answer the questions.

1 Does Jenny have art at nine o'clock?
   Yes, she does.
2 Does Noah have geography at eleven thirty?
   ....
3 Do they have science at a quarter to ten?
   ....
4 Does Noah have music at ten thirty?
   ....
5 Does Jenny have history at eleven thirty?
   ....
6 Does Jenny have English at one fifteen?
   ....

Monday	Noah	Jenny
🕘	math	art
🕘	science	science
🕙	music	math
🕚	history	geography
🕐	computer science	English

★★ 5 Write questions with the Present simple of these verbs. Then answer the questions.

| clean up   get up   go   like   ~~live~~ |

1 you and your family / in a small town?
   Do you and your family live in a small town?
   Yes, we do. / No, we don't.
2 your mom / at 7 a.m.?
   ....
   ....
3 you / your room every day?
   ....
   ....
4 your best friend / animals?
   ....
   ....
5 your parents / to the movies on the weekend?
   ....
   ....

Grammar Reference pages 112–113

Reading

1 **Read the text. Choose the correct description.**

1 Lance goes to school every day. He has classes with the other students in the classroom.

2 Lance doesn't go to school every day. He has classes with the other students on his computer.

The School of the Air

This is Lance. He's Australian. He doesn't go to school because there isn't a school where he lives. Australia is a very big country, and he lives on a sheep farm hundreds of kilometers from a town.

Lance studies at home. He has books, pens and pencils, but his classes are on the computer. Every morning, Lance sits in front of his laptop for an hour, and watches and listens to his classes. His teachers use cameras and interactive whiteboards. He can talk to his teacher and the other students in his "class." In the afternoon, Lance does his homework. He emails his homework to his teachers.

A lot of children live on farms and study at home in Australia. Once a year, the students in each "class" meet. Lance flies to a school in Port Macquarie and stays there for a week. He and the other students go on trips, and there's also a Sports Day. It's a great week, and it's the only time he sees the other students.

2 **Read the text again. Are the statements true (T) or false (F)?**

1 Lance lives on a sheep farm in Australia.   *T*

2 He walks to school every day.   ....

3 The teachers use cameras and interactive whiteboards.   ....

4 He doesn't have any homework.   ....

5 Lance stays at a school in Port Macquarie for two weeks.   ....

6 There's a Sports Day for the class once a year.   ....

3 **Answer the questions.**

1 Why does Lance study at home?
There isn't a school where he lives.

2 Are Lance's classes in the morning?
....

3 Does Lance talk to the other students?
....

4 Does Lance mail his homework to his teachers?
....

5 Do many children study at home in Australia?
....

6 Does Lance fly to Port Macquarie?
....

Listening

1 **Listen to a radio interview. Mark the correct picture.**
13   Where does Darren study?

1 ☐   2 ☐   3 ☐

2 **Listen again. Choose the correct options.**
13   1 Darren *goes / doesn't go* to school.

2 He *has / doesn't have* classes with his parents.

3 He *studies / doesn't study* history.

4 Darren's sisters *play / don't play* the guitar.

5 They *meet / don't meet* other children every week.

3 **Listen again. Complete the sentences.**
13   1 Darren is *13 years old*.

2 Darren studies with his ....

3 Darren studies the same subjects as ....
....

4 His sisters have ....

5 Darren's guitar lesson is on ....

6 Every week, the home-schooled children go to the swimming pool, a museum or ....
....

Writing • An email

Brain Trainer

When there are simple rules, learn them.

Write *in*, *on* and *at* in these rules for time phrases:

_____ + day
_____ + the morning / the evening
_____ + time

Now do Exercise 1.

1 Complete the emails with *in*, *on* or *at*.

New Message ⊗

Send

Hi Chris,

Harry Potter is playing at the movie theater next week. It starts [1] *at* seven o'clock [2] .... the evening. Are you free any day? Let me know, and I can get the tickets.

Fraser

New Message ⊗

Send

Hi Fraser,

Great idea! I can't go [3] .... Monday because I go swimming [4] .... six thirty. [5] .... Tuesday, it's my mom's birthday party [6] .... the evening. I'm free [7] .... Wednesday. I can also go [8] .... Thursday, but I have a guitar lesson [9] .... 5:20 [10] .... Friday. Is Wednesday or Thursday good for you and the others?

Chris

2 Read the emails in Exercise 1. Complete Chris's planner for next week. Then complete it for you.

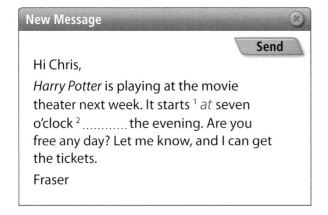

Monday	*swimming / 6:30*
Tuesday	....
Wednesday	....
Thursday	....
Friday	....

Monday	....
Tuesday	....
Wednesday	....
Thursday	....
Friday	....

3 Write sentences about your week. Use your planner from Exercise 2.

1 On Monday, I have a ....
2 On Tuesday, ...
3 ....
4 ....
5 ....

4 Write a short email to Fraser. Use the model in Exercise 1 and your information from Exercises 2 and 3.

Hi Fraser,
Good idea! ....
....
....
....
....
....
....
....
....
....
....

Check 1

Grammar

1 **Choose the correct options.**

0 He *has / have* a party for *our / his* birthday.
1 I *has / have* a new shirt. I love *its / her* color.
2 Tania *has / have* a car. *His / Her* car is red.
3 We *has / have* two laptops at home. They are my *parent's / parents'* laptops.
4 This is *John's / Johns'* wallet. It *doesn't have / don't have* any money in it.
5 My friends *doesn't have / don't have* a big yard. *His / Their* yard is small.

/ 5 points

2 **What's on the table? Write *There's/There isn't*, *There are/There aren't* and *a/an, some* or *any*.**

0 *There are some* comics.
1 .... camera.
2 .... MP3 player.
3 .... books.
4 .... pens.
5 .... watch.

/ 5 points

3 **Look at the information. Answer the questions.**

	Lizzy	Noah
⚽	✓	✗
🩳	✗	✓
⛸	✗	✗
🚲	✓	✓
🎹🎸	✗	✓

0 Can Lizzy juggle?   *Yes, she can.*
1 Can Noah play the piano?
....
2 Can Noah swim?
....
3 Can Noah and Lizzy skate?
....
4 Can Noah and Lizzy bike?
....
5 Can Lizzy play the guitar?
....

/ 5 points

4 **Complete the sentences with the Present simple of the verbs.**

0 We *like* (like) art, and we love (love) music.
1 My sisters .... (not play) tennis in PE. They .... (do) gymnastics.
2 I .... (not wear) a green uniform. I .... (wear) a black uniform.
3 My best friend .... (not bike) to school. She .... (walk).
4 .... Mrs. Bagshaw .... (teach) social studies? No, she ....
5 .... classes .... (end) at ten? Yes, they ....

/ 5 points

Vocabulary

5 **Complete the names of the school subjects (1–5). Then match them to the pictures (a–e).**

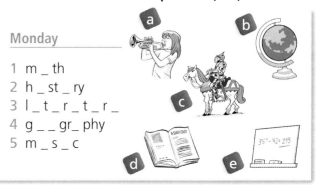

Monday

1 m _ th
2 h _ st _ ry
3 l _ t _ r _ t _ r _
4 g _ _ gr _ phy
5 m _ s _ c

/ 5 points

6 Complete the sentences with places.

0 There are trees in the p*ark*.
1 Let's get a cup of coffee at the c ....
2 There are a lot of old statues in the
m ....
3 Doctors work at the h ....
4 People go to the l ....
to borrow books.
5 There's a swimming pool in the
s .... c ....

/ 5 points

Speaking

7 Match the orders (a–f) to the pictures (1–6). Then complete the orders with these words.

behind   in   in front of   ~~next to~~   on   under

a ☑ 4 Don't play soccer *next to* the street.
b ☐ Don't talk .... the library.
c ☐ Put the bag .... the table.
d ☐ Wait for me .... the movie
theater.
e ☐ Don't stand .... the TV.
f ☐ Walk with me .... the umbrella.

/ 5 points

8 Rewrite the text. Write the times in a different way.

Good morning and welcome to the start of
the new school year.

 The school opens at <u>eight thirty-five</u>.

 The first class starts at <u>nine fifteen</u>.

 The morning break is at <u>ten forty-five</u>.

 Lunch is at <u>twelve thirty</u>.

 The afternoon classes start at <u>two p.m</u>.

 School gets out at <u>three ten</u>.

Good morning and welcome to the start of
the new school year.
0 The school opens *at twenty-five to nine.*
1 The first class starts ....
2 The morning break is ....
3 Lunch is ....
4 The afternoon classes start ....
5 School gets out ....

/ 5 points

Translation

9 Translate the sentences.

1 He doesn't have his dad's laptop.
....
2 There's a big shopping mall in our town.
....
3 I get up at seven thirty, and then I get dressed.
....
4 Do we have a science class on Thursday?
....
5 She can juggle six balls.
....

/ 5 points

Dictation

10 Listen and write.

14

/ 5 points

Animal Magic

Vocabulary • Unusual animals

★ (1) **Label these animals.**

> frog   giant rabbit   hissing cockroach
> ~~piranha~~   pygmy goat

1 *piranha*

3 ....
....

4 ....

10 ....

2 ....
....

5 ....
....

7 ....

9 ....

8 ....

6 ....
....

★ (2) **Put the letters in the correct order. Then label the animals in the picture in Exercise 1.**

6 tsikc secnti   *stick insect*
7 urtaatlan   ....
8 iazrdl   ....
9 aroprt   ....
10 yptohn   ....

★★ (3) **Read the sentences and choose the correct animal.**

1 It's black, and it eats insects.
   (tarantula) / giant rabbit / piranha
2 It's very long, but it can't walk.
   lizard / python / stick insect
3 It's colorful, and it can fly.
   giant rabbit / parrot / lizard
4 It's a farm animal and a popular pet.
   pygmy goat / hissing cockroach / lizard

> **Brain Trainer**
>
> **Learn the common and useful words first. Choose the common word in each pair:**
> *mammal / dog   tarantula / spider*
> *frog / amphibian   fish / piranha*
> **Now do Exercise 4.**

★★ (4) **Complete the table.**

	Category	Animal
1	*amphibian*	frog toad
2	....	parrot
3	mammal	....
4	....	lizard ....
5	insect	....
6	fish	....
7	....	tarantula

★★ (5) **Complete the sentences with these words.**

> frogs   insects   mammals
> parrots   ~~reptiles~~   tarantulas

1 Snakes and lizards are *reptiles*.
2 .... are birds.
3 .... and toads are amphibians.
4 Cockroaches are .... , and they have six legs.
5 .... are spiders, not insects, because they have eight legs.
6 Goats, dogs and cats are all ....

★★ (6) **Complete the dialogue with these words.**

> amphibian ~~animals~~ do do lizard reptile

Paul Do you like ¹ *animals*?
Jen Yes, I ² ....
Paul Do you have a pet?
Jen Yes, I ³ .... I like reptiles. I have a snake and a ⁴ .... I have a frog, too.
Paul Is that a ⁵ ....?
Jen No, it's an ⁶ ....

> **Workbook** page 119

Reading

★ **1** Read the blog. One animal is in the photos but not in the blog. Put an ✕ next to the photo.

★ **2** Read the text again. Are the statements true (T) or false (F)?

1 The school is in a big city. F
2 There are cows on the farm. ....
3 Susie is eleven years old. ....
4 Susie usually helps with the goats. ....
5 The farm sells the eggs and meat. ....
6 Her favorite animals are the pigs. ....

★ **3** Choose the correct options.

1 There are eighty (sheep) / pigs on the farm.
2 The farm has two dogs / donkeys.
3 Susie is in sixth grade / seventh grade.
4 She likes / doesn't like the classes on the farm.
5 She likes the eggs / chickens.
6 The horses are old / big.

★★ **4** Answer the questions.

1 Where is the school?
  It's in the country.
2 How many goats are there?
  ....
3 When are Susie's classes on the farm?
  ....
4 What does Susie learn about on the farm?
  ....
5 Why does Susie go to school early?
  ....
6 How does Susie help with the chickens?
  ....

Blog

My school isn't in a town. It's in the country. It's a special school because it has a farm. There are eighty sheep, seventeen cows, eight pigs, four goats, a lot of chickens, two horses and two donkeys on the school farm.

My name's Susie. I'm eleven, and I'm in 6th grade. This is my first year at the school. Every Tuesday we have a class on the farm. We learn about the animals and how to take care of them. I really like the classes. I often go to school early to help on the farm because I want to work with animals when I grow up. I usually help with the chickens. Some days I feed the chickens and give them clean water. On other days, I clean the enclosure and collect the eggs. We sell the eggs and meat. I like the chickens and pigs, but my favorite animals are the horses. They're big, but very friendly!

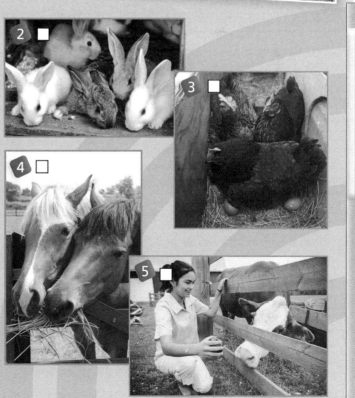

Grammar • Adverbs of frequency

★ **(1)** **Write the words in the correct place.**

always	hardly ever	~~never~~
often	sometimes	usually

0%   25%   50% 60%   80%   100%

1 0%   *never*
2 25%   ....
3 50%   ....
4 60%   ....
5 80%   ....
6 100%   ....

★ **(2)** **Read the text. Write *Bob* or *Will* next to each picture.**

Bob   ....

....

....

Bob and Will are friends, but they are very different. Bob always gets up early and takes a shower. He sometimes eats cereal for breakfast, and sometimes toast and honey. After breakfast, Bob feeds the cat. He always leaves the house at eight thirty and takes the bus to school. He's never late.

Will hardly ever gets up early, and he never takes a shower in the morning. He always eats cereal for breakfast. He never eats toast and honey. After breakfast, Will sometimes feeds the fish. He usually leaves the house at eight forty and often misses the bus to school. He's often late.

Grammar Reference pages 114–115

Brain Trainer

Always check the word order in your sentences. Remember:

Subject + adverb of frequency + verb
We   never   go to the theater.
but
Subject + verb *to be* + adverb of frequency
He   's   hardly ever late.

Now do Exercise 3.

★★ **(3)** **Rewrite the sentences with an adverb of frequency. Make the sentences true for you.**

1 I eat breakfast in the morning.
....
2 I'm late for school.
....
3 I help at home.
....
4 I go to the park after school.
....

★★ **(4)** **Put the words in the correct order to make sentences. What does Penny do on the weekend?**

1 never / She / volleyball / plays
She never plays volleyball.
2 often / Sunday / on / TV / watches / She
....
3 sometimes / the / She / movies / goes / to
....
4 always / on / talks / phone / She / to / friends / her / the
....
5 usually / homework / she / her / do / Does ?
....

★★ **(5)** **Write sentences and questions. Put the adverb of frequency in the correct place.**

1 The parrot / talk / to me (often)
The parrot often talks to me.
2 Visitors / be / scared of the spiders (sometimes)
....
3 Our dog / get / on my bed (never)
....
4 She / feed / the cat (always)
....
5 you / clean / the rabbit enclosure? (usually)
....

Grammar • Present simple with *Wh* questions

★ **(1)** **Read the answers. Choose the correct question words.**

1 *Who / (Where)* is your teacher?
   She's in the library.
2 *Why / How often* do you have English classes?
   We have three classes a week.
3 *Who / What* do you sit next to in class?
   I sit next to Amelia.
4 *How often / Why* are you late?
   Because I missed the bus.
5 *What / When* does the zookeeper feed
   the rabbits?   He gives them carrots.

★ **(2)** **Complete the questions with these words.**

| How often   What   When   Where   ~~Who~~ |

1 *Who* is your science teacher?
2 .... homework do you have today?
3 .... do penguins live?
4 .... does the movie start?
5 .... do you play sports?

★ **(3)** **Write the questions.**

1 What animals / you / like?
   What animals do you like?
2 Who / scared of spiders?
   ....
3 How often / you / take your dog for a walk?
   ....
4 Where / pythons / come from?
   ....
5 When / the zookeeper / feed the rabbits?
   ....

★ **(4)** **Write the questions for these answers.**

1 *What is your favorite football team?*
   My favorite football team is the Cowboys.
2 ....
   My English teacher is Ms. Barber.
3 ....
   My school is next to the park.
4 ....
   My birthday is June 26.
5 ....
   My teacher is hardly ever out of town.

Grammar Reference pages 114–115

Vocabulary • Parts of the body

★ **(1)** **Match the pictures to the descriptions.**

1 It has a small head. It has three black
   paws and one white paw. It has a long tail.   *d*
2 It has a long white neck, white wings,
   an orange beak and black feet.
3 It has a small head, six thin legs and a
   long, thin tail, but it doesn't have wings.
4 It has two arms and legs. It has two hands
   and feet. It has ten fingers and toes.

★ **(2)** **Match the sentence halves 1–5 to a–e.**

1 A lizard has   a four paws.
2 A tarantula has   b two wings and a beak.
3 A rabbit has   c fins.
4 A parrot has   d a long tail.
5 A fish has   e eight legs and feet.

★★ **(3)** **Put the letters in the correct order.**

1 A python has a long body and a small *head*
   (deha), but it doesn't have a *neck* (knce).
2 We have ten .... (nifgsre)
   and ten .... (oste).
3 Fish have a body, ...
   (nifs) and a .... (lait).
4 Parrots have a .... (akbe)
   and colorful .... (sigwn).
5 Dogs have four ....
   (gels) and .... (waps).

★★★ **(4)** **Write about yourself using these words.**

arms	feet	fingers	hands	head
legs	neck	toes	wings	

I have ....
....
....
....
....
....

Workbook page 119

Chatroom Likes and dislikes

Speaking and Listening

★ **1** **Mark the sentences about likes.**

1 That dog's very dirty. ☐
2 Rex hates taking a shower. ☐
3 He loves running around the yard. ☐
4 He doesn't like swimming. ☐
5 He likes hiding things. ☐
6 He's a very friendly dog. ☐

★ **2** **Read and listen to the conversation.**
15 **Mark the things Rex likes.**

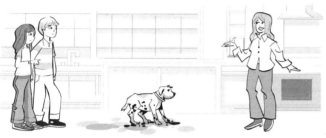

Beth Hi, Mom. I'm back. Frank's here, too.
Mom Hello, Frank. The dog's very dirty, Beth.
Can you clean him, please?
Beth But Mom, Rex hates getting a bath.
Mom I know, but he can go outside after his
bath. He loves running around the yard.
Beth Rex hates water. He doesn't like swimming,
and he never goes in the river.
Frank Does he like playing with a ball?
Beth No, not really. He likes hiding things.
He often hides our stuff in the yard.
Frank He's a very friendly dog.
Beth Yes. He likes sitting next to me in the evening.

1 ☐   2 ☐   3 ☐

4 ☐   5 ☐   6 ☐

★★ **3** **Complete the conversation with these words.**
16 **Then listen and check.**

cook	eat	play sports
play tennis	run	watch TV

Ali What do you like doing in your free time?
Liz I love ¹ 🎾 *playing tennis*.
Ali So do I. I like ² 🏃 .... ,
too.
Mia I don't like ³ 🏀⚽ ....
I like ⁴ 📺 ....
Ali You like ⁵ 🍲 .... , too.
I love ⁶ 🛒 .... your
food.
Mia That's true. Thank you, Ali.

★★ **4** **Write true sentences about yourself. Use *love*,
like, *don't like* and *hate*.**

1 bike
....
2 eat eggs
....
3 watch sports on TV
....
4 listen to music
....
5 clean up my room
....

★★ **5** **Look at the table. Write a conversation between
★ Jo and Simon. Use the model in Exercise 3.**

	Likes	Doesn't like
Jo	biking	reading
	going to the movies	
	listening to music	
Simon	biking	listening to music
	reading	singing
	running	

Speaking and Listening page 123

Grammar • Must/Mustn't

★ **(1)** **Match the pictures (1–3) to the rules (a–f).**

1 [c] [ ]

2 [ ] [ ]

3 [ ] [ ]

a You mustn't run across the street.
b You mustn't go to school.
c You must stay in bed.
d You must be quiet.
e You must look left and right.
f You mustn't write in the books.

★ **(2)** **Complete the sentences with *must* or *mustn't*.**

1 We *mustn't* arrive late for school.
2 They .... be good to animals.
3 He .... hurt other people.
4 You .... shout at the children.

★★ **(3)** **Put the words in the correct order. Then answer the question below.**

1 late / You / be / mustn't
   You mustn't be late.
2 the / mustn't / classroom / eat / in / He
   ....
3 a / They / wear / uniform / must
   ....
4 phones / use / mustn't / cell / our / We
   ....
5 She / listen / teacher / to / must / the
   ....
   Where are they?   ....
   ....

★★ **(4)** **Complete the sentences with these phrases and *must* or *mustn't*.**

buy a ticket	clean up my room	close the gates
~~litter~~	stand on her desk	talk

1 You *mustn't litter* in the park. ✖
2 They ....
   on the farm. ✔
3 We ....
   in the library. ✖
4 She ....
   at school. ✖
5 I ....
   at home. ✔
6 You ....
   on the bus. ✔

★★ **(5)** **Write sentences about the park rules. Use a word or phrase from each box.**

You	must mustn't	~~pick~~ write climb keep put	the trees. on the statues. ~~the flowers.~~ your dog on a leash. litter in a trash can.

1 *You mustn't pick the flowers.*
2 ....
3 ....
4 ....
5 ....

Grammar Reference pages 114–115

Reading

1 **Read the article quickly. Choose the correct answer.**

What does Jack Stone do? He's a …
a zookeeper.   b photographer.
c teacher.   d farmer.

Jack Stone doesn't have a pet, but he has a lot of pictures of animals because he's a photographer. He takes photos of pets. He is very good, and his photos are often in the newspapers. He also has photos on his website. There are a lot of cats and dogs, but there are other pets too—horses, rabbits, guinea pigs, parrots and fish.

Jack explains, "People usually bring their pet to my studio, but sometimes I go to the pet's home to take the photos. I like the pets to be happy, or the photos aren't good. I often take the photos outside because animals like being outside. I like finding the right place to photograph the animal. People want photos because they love their pets. Every pet is special. I show their character. My photos show how each animal is different. I like animals, and I like taking photos. I'm lucky because I love my work."

2 **Read the article again. Are the statements true (T) or false (F)?**

1 Jack has a lot of cats.	*F*
2 Jack's photos are never in the newspapers.	....
3 Jack only takes photos of cats and dogs.	....
4 Jack doesn't always take the photos in his studio.	....
5 Jack wants the pets to be happy.	....
6 Jack hates taking photos.	....

3 **Answer the questions.**

1 What does Jack take photos of?
He takes photos of pets.
2 Where can you see Jack's photos?
....
3 Which animals can you see on his website?
....
4 Where does Jack take the photos?
....

Listening

1 **Listen and mark the correct picture.**

17   1 ☐   2 ☐   3 ☐

2 **Listen again. Choose the correct answers.**

17   1 Every day, Ben takes a photo of a different *child / animal.*
2 The unusual pet on his website is a *stick insect / frog.*
3 There's a funny photo of a *tarantula / parrot.*
4 The animals hardly ever *run away / bite.*
5 Ben's favorite photo is of a *goat / python.*

3 **Read the answers and write the questions.**
17   **Then listen again and check.**

> Are there any funny photos?
> Are there any unusual pets on your website?
> Do the animals bite you?
> What's your favorite photo?
> ~~Are there people in the photos?~~

1 *Are there people in the photos?*
Not usually.
2 ....
Yes. There's a photo of a red frog on a twig.
3 ....
Yes, there are. The photo of a tarantula on a man's head is funny.
4 ....
Hardly ever.
5 ....
It's a photo of a goat.

Writing • An animal fact sheet

1 Look at the fact sheet and complete the sentences.

Pet Fact Sheet | **Stick Insects**

Continent: South America, Asia, Australia
Weight: 65 g
Length: 17 cm
Habitat: trees
Diet: plants, leaves
Abilities: can hide very well

1 Stick insects come from *South America, Asia and Australia.*
2 They grow to .... long, and they weigh ....
3 They live in ....
4 They eat ....
5 They can ....

2 Complete the description with these words.

apples	backyard	cats	eats	eyes
lives	~~pet~~		sunny	white

3 Complete the table for Emma. Use the information in Exercise 2.

Name	Emma	Polly
Type of animal	¹ *guinea pig*	parrot
Home	²	cage
Diet	³	bird seed, nuts, fruit
Color	⁴	gray beak, red head and body, blue and yellow wings
Likes & dislikes	⁵	• likes talking and listening to people • doesn't like going to bed late

4 Write a short article about Polly. Use the model from Exercise 2 and the notes in Exercise 3.

....
....
....
....
....
....
....

My pet's home _____

My ¹ *pet* is a guinea pig. Her name is Emma, and she ² .... in a hutch in the ³ ....

Diet _____

She usually ⁴ .... special guinea pig food. I sometimes give her ⁵ .... , too.

Appearance _____

She's brown and ⁶ .... She has small ⁷ .... and ears, and a pink nose.

Likes and dislikes _____

She likes ⁸ .... days because she can run around outside. She doesn't like ⁹ .... because they want to eat her!

Check 2

Grammar

1 Write the rules. Use *You must* or *You mustn't*.

> • tell someone where you are going ✓
> • walk on your own ✗
> • take food and water ✓
> • go in foggy weather ✗
> • take a map ✓

Rules for hiking in the mountains

0 *You must tell someone where you are going.*
1 ....
2 ....
3 ....
4 ....

/ 4 points

2 Complete the sentences with the Present simple or Present continuous.

0 We often *go* (go) to the zoo in the summer.
1 .... you .... (wear) your hat now?
2 Why .... they always ....
(get up) early?
3 When .... he usually ....
(finish) school?
4 .... she .... (do) gymnastics now?
5 We .... (not play) tennis on Sundays.
6 I ....(watch) a news show at the moment.

/ 6 points

3 Choose the correct options. Then complete the text with *much* or *many*.

How much food do we have? There ⁰(*isn't*)/
aren't much pasta, and there ¹ *isn't* / *aren't*
.... shrimp. There ² *isn't* / *aren't*
.... broccoli, and there ³ *isn't* / *aren't*
.... carrots. There ⁴ *is* / *are* a lot of eggs,
but there ⁵ *isn't* / *aren't* .... ice cream.

/ 5 points

4 Look at the pictures. Complete the sentences with these phrases. Then put the word in parentheses in the correct place.

go ice skating	~~go kayaking~~
go mountain biking	go rollerblading
go climbing	play the guitar

0 (often) He *often goes kayaking* when it's sunny.
1 (never) She ....
when it's foggy.
2 (always) They ....
when it's cloudy.
3 (usually) He ....
when it's raining.
4 (hardly ever) He ....
when it's windy.
5 (sometimes) They ....
when it's cold.

/ 5 points

Vocabulary

5 Look at the pictures and complete the sentences.

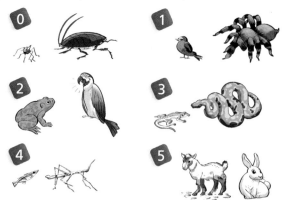

/ 5 points

0 The *spider* is smaller than the *hissing cockroach.*
1 The .... is larger than the ....
2 The .... is noisier than the ....
3 The .... is longer than the ....
4 The .... is smaller than the ....
5 The .... is dirtier than the ....

/ 5 points

6 Label the pizzas.

0 b*anana* pizza
1 c .... and h .... pizza
2 t .... and s .... pizza
3 c .... and t .... pizza
4 s .... and b .... pizza
5 s .... and e .... pizza

/ 5 points

Speaking

7 Match the sentences (1–5) to the responses (a–e).

0 I have the best grades in the class!   0
1 Do you like kayaking?
2 The football game isn't on TV today.
3 I have tickets for *X Factor* next week.
4 I can hear an insect. Can you see it?
5 I like dancing.

0 Wow! That's wonderful! Good job!
a How amazing! Lucky you!
b Me too! I love it.
c No. I don't like water sports.
d Yes. It's just a mosquito.
e Really? Oh! Why not?

/ 5 points

8 Choose the correct options to complete the conversation.

Waiter   Are you ready to order?
Mom   Yes, we are.
Waiter   What ⁰ *would you like* / *do you want*?
Sarah   ¹ *Give me / I'll have* the spaghetti, please.
Mom   And ² *I'd like / I want* the burger with fries, please.
Waiter   ³ *What do you want / Would you like anything* to drink?
Sarah   ⁴ *Can I have / Give me* a glass of orange juice, please?
Mom   And ⁵ *I drink / I'd like* water, please.
Waiter   Yes, of course. Is that all?
Mom   Yes, thank you.

/ 5 points

Translation

9 Translate the sentences.

1 She hardly ever goes hiking in winter.
....
....

2 Are they feeding the rabbits?
....
....

3 How much bread do we have in the fridge?
....
....

4 Autumn is usually foggier than spring.
....
....

5 You must be quiet in the library.
....
....

/ 5 points

Dictation

10 Listen and write.
25

/ 5 points

Grammar Reference ①

• Have

Affirmative		
I/You/We/They	have	ice skates.
He/She/It	has	a magazine.

Negative		
I/You/We/They	don't have (do not have)	an MP3 player.
He/She/It	doesn't have (does not have)	a skateboard.

Questions and short answers	
Do I/you/we/they have a laptop?	Yes, I/you/we/they do. No, I/you/we/they don't.
Does he/she/it have a cell phone?	Yes, he/she/it does. No, he/she/it doesn't.

Use

- We use *have* to talk about possession.
  You have a lot of books.
  He has a blue backpack.

Form

- To form the affirmative, we use subject + *have/has*.
  *They **have** a camera.*
  *She **has** a poster of The Killers in her bedroom.*

- To form the negative, we add *don't* or *doesn't* before *have*.
  *I **don't have** a watch. (don't = do not)*
  *The car **doesn't have** a radio. (doesn't = does not)*

- The word order changes in questions:
  Do/Does + subject + have.
  ***Do** you **have** the comics?*
  ***Does** he **have** a laptop?*

- In short answers, we do not repeat *have*.
  A *Do they have a game console?*
  B *Yes, they do.*
  A *Does she have a guitar?*
  B *No, she doesn't.*

Common mistakes

He has an MP3 player. ✓
He have an MP3 player. ✗
They don't have any posters. ✓
They not have any posters. ✗

• Possessive adjectives and Possessive 's

Possessive adjectives		Possessive 's
I	my	**One person**
you	your	Paula's cat.
he	his	John's wallet.
she	her	**Two or more people**
it	its	My parents' house.
we	our	Dave and Jack's room.
they	their	

Use

We use possessive adjectives and the possessive 's to say who things belong to.

*It's **my** backpack.*
***Sam's** skateboard is green.*

Form

- We use possessive adjectives before a noun: possessive adjective + noun.
  *It's **their** dog.*

- We use **'s** after a singular noun.
  *Penny**'s** watch   my mom**'s** car*

- We use **'** after a plural noun ending in **-s**.
  *My cousins**'** house*

- We use **'s** after a plural noun not ending in **-s**.
  *the children**'s** backpacks*

Common mistake

It's Dave and Jack's room. ✓
It's Dave's and Jack's room. ✗

Grammar practice • Have

1 **Rewrite the sentences. Use full forms.**

1 I don't have a poster of Katy Perry.
   I do not have a poster of Katy Perry.
2 She doesn't have a camera.
   ....
3 We don't have a big house.
   ....
4 He doesn't have a collection of *Star Wars* posters.
   ....
5 They don't have a lot of magazines.
   ....
6 The classroom doesn't have white walls.
   ....

2 **Complete the sentences with *have* or *has*.**

1 I *have* a big family.
2 She .... two sisters and a brother.
3 My cousin .... a black and white cat.
4 You .... a really cool hat!
5 Tracey .... long brown hair.
6 The dog .... brown eyes.

3 **Look and write sentences. Use the correct form of *have*.**

1 Eve / cell phone / MP3 player
   Eve has a cell phone. She doesn't have an MP3 player.
2 Maria and Julia / magazine / book
   ....
3 Martin / soccer ball / skateboard
   ....
4 Ben and Leo / drinks / food
   ....

• Possessive adjectives

4 **Write questions using *have* and the correct possessive adjective. Then write the answers.**

1 he / guitar ✗
   Does he have his guitar? No, he doesn't.
2 you / new CD ✓
   ....
   ....
3 the fans / cameras ✗
   ....
   ....
4 the girl / autograph book ✓
   ....
   ....
5 we / tickets for the concert ✓
   ....
   ....

• Possessive 's

5 **Choose the correct options.**

1 It's their *parent's* / *parents'* car.
2 They're my *cousin's* / *cousins'* cats.
3 They're *John's* / *Johns'* pencils.
4 It's *Mr. Black's* / *Mr. Blacks'* newspaper.
5 It's our *dog's* / *dogs'* ball.

Grammar Reference

• There is/There are; Some/Any

Singular	Plural
Affirmative	
There's (There is) a child in the park.	There are some children in the park.
Negative	
There isn't (There is not) a café in the town square.	There aren't (There are not) any cafés in the town square.
Questions and short answers	
Is there a poster on the wall?	Yes, there is. No, there isn't (there is not).
Are there any posters on the wall?	Yes, there are. No, there aren't (there are not).

Use

- We use *There is/There are* to say something exists, and *There isn't/There aren't* to say something does not exist.

- We use *There's* and *There isn't* with singular nouns.
  There's a museum next to the bank.
  There isn't a library.

- We use *There are* and *There aren't* with plural nouns.
  There are twenty stores in the mall.
  There aren't any trains today.

- We use *some* in affirmative sentences.
  There are **some** tickets for the concert.

- We use *any* in negative sentences and questions.
  There aren't **any** books in my backpack.
  Are there **any** strawberries in the fridge?

Form

- To form the affirmative, we use *There + is/are*.
  There's a swimming pool in the sports complex.
  There are some beautiful parks in the city.

- To form the negative, we add *not* after *There is/are*.
  There isn't a café at the station. (= There is not)
  There aren't any French students in our class.
  (= There are not)

- The word order changes in questions: *Is/Are + there*.
  Is there a hospital near here?
  Are there any keys on the table?

• Can/Can't for ability

Affirmative		
I/You/He/She/It/We/They	can	juggle.
Negative		
I/You/He/She/It/We/They	can't (cannot)	dance.
Questions and short answers		
Can I/you/he/she/it/we/they skate?	Yes, I/you/he/she/it/we/they can. No, I/you/he/she/it/we/they can't (cannot).	

Use

- We use *can* to talk about ability.
  I can play the guitar.
  He can't ride a bike.

Form

- To form the affirmative, we use *can* + main verb.
  We can swim.

- To form the negative, we add *not* after *can*.
  The short form of *cannot* is *can't*.
  She can't dance.

- The word order changes in questions:
  Can + subject + main verb.
  Can you sing?

- In short answers, we do not repeat the main verb.
  A *Can it fly?* **B** *Yes, it can.*

Grammar practice • There is/ There are; Some/Any

1 Match the stores (A–D) to the descriptions (1–3). Complete the descriptions with *There is/isn't* or *There are/aren't*.

1 ☐ In this store, you can buy furniture.
  ¹ *There are* some tables and chairs.
  ² .... a big desk, but
  ³ .... any beds.

2 ☐ In this store, ⁴ .... a lot of DVDs. ⁵ .... a lot of CDs too, but ⁶ .... any DVD or CD players.

3 ☐ In this store, ⁷ .... a lot of toys. ⁸ .... a tepee and a kite, but ⁹ .... a bike.

2 Complete the description of the fourth picture.

books	computer	interactive whiteboard
magazines	~~pens~~	

In this store, there are a lot of ¹ *pens* and
² .... , but there aren't any
³ .... There's a
⁴ .... , but there isn't an
⁵ ....

3 Answer the questions about the pictures in Exercise 1.

1 Is there a computer in one of the stores?
  Yes, there is.
2 Is there a girl in the DVD store?
  ....
3 Are there any children in the toy store?
  ....
4 Are there any people in the furniture store?
  ....

4 Write sentences using *There is/are* or *There isn't/aren't*.

1 mountains / my country ✓
  There are some mountains in my country.
2 museum / my town ✗
  ....
3 library / my school ✓
  ....
4 pets / my house ✗
  ....

• Can/Can't for ability

5 Match the sentences (1–4) to the people.

	⛸	🏊	🤹	🚲	🎾
Andrew	✗	✓	✗	✓	✗
Ben	✓	✓	✗	✓	✓
Charlie	✗	✗	✗	✓	✓
Dave	✗	✓	✓	✓	✓

1 He can't skate, but he can juggle and bike.
  Dave
2 He can skate and play tennis, but he can't juggle.
3 He can swim and bike, but he can't play tennis.
4 He can bike and play tennis, but he can't swim.

6 Answer the questions about the people in Exercise 5.

1 Who can juggle? *Dave*
2 Who can't play tennis? ....
3 Who can't swim? ....
4 Who can skate? ....
5 What can they all do? ....

7 Answer the questions with full sentences.

1 Who can drive in your family?
  My mom and dad can drive.
2 What water sports can you do?
  ....
3 What languages can you speak?
  ....
4 What musical instrument can you play?
  ....

Grammar Reference ③

• Present simple: affirmative and negative

Affirmative		
I/You/We/They	start	school at 9 a.m.
He/She/It	gets up	early.
Negative		
I/You/We/They	don't (do not)	take a shower in the morning.
He/She/It	doesn't (does not)	go to bed early.

Time expressions

every day
every Monday
on the weekend
after school
on Mondays
at nine o'clock

Use

We use the Present simple to talk about:

* routines and habits.
  *He **gets up** at 7 a.m. every day.*

* things that are true in general.
  *We **live** in a small town.*

Form

* To form the third person singular (with *he, she* and *it*), we add **-s**, **-es** or **-ies** to the verb. (See **Spelling rules**.)
  *She speak**s** Spanish.*

* To form the negative, we use *do not (don't)* with *I, you, we* and *they*. We use *does not (doesn't)* with *he, she* and *it*.
  *We **don't** have dinner together.*
  *He **doesn't** do Sudoku puzzles.*

* We use time expressions to say when or how often we do something.
  *She plays soccer **on Saturdays**.*

* The time expression usually goes at the end of the sentence.
  *Eric goes to bed **at 9:30 p.m.***

• Spelling rules: verb + -s

most verbs: add **-s**	read → reads play → plays
verbs that end in **-ss**, **-ch**, **-sh**, **-x** and **-o**: add **-es**	kiss → kisses watch → watches wash → washes fix → fixes go → goes
verbs that end in a consonant + **y**: drop the **y** and add **-ies**	study → studies

Common mistakes

He goes to bed early. ✓
~~He go to bed early.~~ ✗
She doesn't eat pizza. ✓
~~She doesn't eats pizza.~~ ✗

• Present simple: questions and short answers

Questions and short answers	
Do I/you/we/they live downtown?	Yes, I/you/we/they do. No, I/you/we/they don't.
Does he/she/it like music?	Yes, he/she/it does. No, he/she/it doesn't.
Negative		
I/You/We/They	don't (do not)	take a shower in the morning.
He/She/It	doesn't (does not)	go to bed early.

Form

* To form questions, we use *do* with *I, you, we* and *they*. We use *does* with *he, she* and *it*. The word order also changes: *Do/Does* + subject + main verb.
  ***Do** they **walk** to school?*
  ***Does** she **speak** English?*

* In short answers, we do not repeat the main verb.
  A ***Does** he **brush** his teeth in the morning?*
  B *Yes, he **does**.*

Common mistake

A *Does he play the guitar?* **B** *Yes, he does.* ✓
A *Does he play the guitar?* **B** *~~Yes, he plays.~~* ✗

Grammar practice • Present simple: affirmative and negative

1 Complete the sentences. Use the Present simple of the verbs and these words.

> her homework   my friends   ~~our teeth~~
> tennis   TV

1 We *brush our teeth* (brush) after breakfast.
2 They .... (play) every day.
3 She .... (do) at home.
4 He .... (watch) in the evening.
5 I .... (meet) in the park.

2 Complete the text. Use the Present simple of the verbs.

I ¹ *like* (like) geography a lot because we
² .... (learn) about other countries.
Our project this year is about South America.
People ³ .... (speak) Spanish in many
South American countries. My mom
⁴ .... (come) from South America,
but she ⁵ .... (not speak) Spanish
because she's Brazilian. The people in Brazil
⁶ .... (not speak) Spanish. They
⁷ .... (speak) Portuguese.

3 Look at the pictures. Correct the sentences.

1 Barry gets up at eight o'clock.
Barry doesn't get up at eight o'clock.
He gets up at seven o'clock.
2 He has breakfast with his dad.

....

3 He bikes to school.

....

4 Classes start at ten o'clock.

....

4 Rewrite the sentences for you. Make them true.

Isabelle

1 Isabelle goes to school by bus.
I go to school by car.
I don't go to school by bus.
2 She likes math.

....
....

3 She watches TV in bed.

....
....

4 She doesn't get up early on the weekend.

....
....

• Present simple: questions and short answers

5 Put the words in the correct order to make questions.

1 at / open / half past nine? / Does / library / the
Does the library open at half past nine?
2 their / Mimi and Noah / friends / meet / school? / Do / after

.... ?

3 Thursdays? / Do / science / have / they / on

.... ?

4 his / clean up / Does / room / he / the / weekend? / on

.... ?

5 go / Does / to / before / sister / bed / your / you?

.... ?

6 Write questions. Then answer the questions for you.

1 you (bike) to school in the morning
Do you bike to school in the morning?
Yes, I do./No, I don't.
2 students (study) computer science at your school

.... ?
....

3 your school day (start) at 8 a.m.

.... ?
....

4 you (wear) a uniform

.... ?
....

Grammar Reference

• Adverbs of frequency

0%		50%			100%
never	hardly ever	sometimes	often	usually	always

I always get up at 6:30.
I hardly ever watch TV.
I am sometimes very tired.

Use

• We often use adverbs of frequency with the Present simple to say how often we do something.
  I **always** do my homework.

• Adverbs of frequency usually go:

  – before the main verb.
  Goats **sometimes** climb trees.

  – after the verb *to be*.
  My dog is **never** sad.

Common mistakes

I never play soccer. ✓
I play never soccer. ✗
She's always tired. ✓
Always she is tired. ✗

• Present simple with *Wh* questions

Wh questions
Where do you live?   In Mexico.
When does the movie end?   At nine o'clock.
What does she eat for lunch?   Sandwiches.
Who do you meet on the way to school?   Lauren and Wendy.
Why does he get up late?   Because he works at night.
How often do they go to the movies?   Every week!

Use

• We use *where* to ask about place.
  Where is the train station?

• We use *when* to ask about time.
  When does the party start?

• We use *what* to ask about things.
  What do you have in your bag?

• We use *who* to ask about people.
  Who can juggle six balls?

• We use *why* to ask the reason for something.
  Why are you late?

• We use *how often* to ask how frequently something happens.
  How often do you clean up your room?

Form

• To form questions with most verbs, we use this word order: *Wh* question word + *do/does* + subject + main verb.
  What does she like?

• To form questions with *to be* and modal verbs, we use inversion.
  Where are you?
  What can she do?

Common mistakes

When do you go to bed? ✓
When you go to bed? ✗
When go you to bed? ✗

• Must/Mustn't

Affirmative		
I/You/He/She/It/We/They	must	listen to her.
Negative		
I/You/He/She/It/We/They	mustn't (must not)	use cell phones in class.

Use

• We use *must* to talk about important rules.
  I **must** do my homework.

• We use *mustn't* to talk about things we are not allowed to do.
  You **mustn't** eat in class.

Form

• To form the affirmative, we use subject + *must* + main verb.
  They **must** keep the dog on a leash.

• To form the negative, we add *not* after *must*.
  They **mustn't** use cell phones in class. (= must not)

Common mistakes

You mustn't play soccer in the park. ✓
You mustn't to play soccer in the park. ✗
You mustn't talking in the library. ✗

Grammar practice • Adverbs of frequency

1 Look at the information in the table. Write the correct name next to each sentence.

Will	20%	50%	50%	60%	100%
Zoe	0%	20%	60%	20%	100%
Luke	100%	0%	60%	0%	80%

1 I never feed the fish.   *Zoe*
2 I sometimes go horseback riding.   ....
3 I hardly ever clean out the rabbits' hutch.   ....
4 I usually take the dog for a walk.   ....
5 I often play with the cat.   ....
6 I always give the fish some food.   ....

2 Look at the information in Exercise 1. Answer the questions with full sentences.

1 How often does Will feed the fish?
  He hardly ever feeds the fish.
2 How often do Luke and Zoe go horseback riding?
  ....
3 How often does Luke play with the cat?
  ....
4 How often does Will clean out the rabbits' hutch?
  ....
5 How often do Zoe and Will take the dog for a walk?
  ....

• Present simple with *Wh* questions

3 Circle the question words. Then translate them.

1 Who ....
2 Where ....
3 Have ....
4 Will ....
5 When ....
6 White ....
7 What ....
8 How ....
9 Has ....
10 Why ....

4 Match the question words (1–6) to the question endings (a–f). Then choose the correct options.

1 Who *f*   a *is / does* the movie start?
2 When   b *is / does* the sports complex?
3 How often   c *are / do* your favorite subjects?
4 Why   d *are / do* you go shopping?
5 What   e *isn't / doesn't* your dog here?
6 Where   f (*is*)/ *do* your favorite actor?

• Must/Mustn't

5 Complete the sentences.

clean up my room	close the gates
eat in class	hurt the animals
jump on my bed	listen to the teacher

1 At home, I must ....
  I mustn't ....
2 At school, we must ....
  We mustn't ....
3 On a farm, you must ....
  You mustn't ....

6 Look at the pictures. Write sentences using *must/mustn't*.

wear / warm clothes	stand under / tree
~~swim / ocean~~	walk / mountains

In bad weather:

1 *You mustn't swim in the ocean.*
2 ....
  ....

3 ....
  ....
4 ....
  ....

Vocabulary

My World

Unit vocabulary

1 Translate the words.

Objects

camera ....

cell phone ....

comics ....

DVD ....

game console ....

guitar ....

ice skates ....

laptop ....

magazine ....

MP3 player ....

poster ....

skateboard ....

wallet ....

watch ....

2 Translate the words.

Adjectives

bad ....

big ....

boring ....

cheap ....

difficult ....

easy ....

expensive ....

good ....

interesting ....

new ....

old ....

popular ....

small ....

unpopular ....

Vocabulary extension

3 Match the photos to the words in the box. Use your dictionary if necessary. Write the words in English and in your language.

| alarm clock | bike helmet | ~~bracelets~~ | hairbrush | keys |

1 ....*bracelets*........ ....

2 ....

3 ....

4 ....

5 ....
....

Vocabulary

Around Town

Unit vocabulary

1 Translate the words.

Places in a town

bank ....

bus station ....

café ....

hospital ....

library ....

movie theater

....

museum ....

park ....

police station

....

post office ....

shopping mall

....

sports complex ....

town square ....

train station ....

2 Translate the words.

Action verbs

bike ....

climb ....

dance ....

fly ....

juggle ....

jump ....

play ....

run ....

sing ....

skate ....

swim ....

walk ....

Vocabulary extension

3 Match the photos to the words in the box. Use your dictionary if necessary. Write the words in English and in your language.

| art gallery | ~~bookstore~~ | restaurant | supermarket | theater |

1 _bookstore_ ....   2 ....

3 ....   4 ....

5 ....
....

Vocabulary ③

Unit vocabulary

1 **Translate the phrases.**

Daily routines

brush my teeth

....

clean up my room

....

do homework ....

get dressed ....

get up ....

go home ....

go to bed ....

have breakfast ....

have dinner ....

have lunch ....

meet friends ....

start school ....

take a shower ....

watch TV ....

2 **Translate the words and phrases.**

School subjects

art ....

computer science

....

English ....

French ....

geography ....

history ....

literature ....

math ....

music ....

PE (physical education)

....

science ....

social studies ....

Vocabulary extension

3 **Match the photos to the words in the box. Use your dictionary if necessary. Write the words in English and in your language.**

| bell | lunch box | pencil case | ~~schedule~~ | textbook |

1 ....*schedule*.... ....

2 ....

3 ....

4 ....

5 ....
....

Vocabulary

Animal Magic

Unit vocabulary

1 Translate the words.

Unusual animals

frog ....

giant rabbit ....

hissing cockroach

....

lizard ....

parrot ....

piranha ....

pygmy goat ....

python ....

stick insect ....

tarantula ....

amphibian ....

bird ....

fish ....

insect ....

mammal ....

reptile ....

spider ....

2 Translate the words.

Parts of the body

arm ....

beak ....

fin ....

finger ....

foot ....

hand ....

head ....

leg ....

neck ....

paw ....

tail ....

toe ....

wing ....

Vocabulary extension

3 Match the photos to the words in the box. Use your dictionary if necessary. Write the words in English and in your language.

| eagle | ladybug | ~~shark~~ | squirrel | turtle |

1 ..... *shark* .... 2 ....

3 .... 4 ....

5 ....
....

Speaking and Listening

Talking about position

• Speaking

1 Look at the pictures and complete the conversations
39 with these words. Then listen and check.

behind	in	in front of	next to
on	under	~~Where~~	

A ¹ *Where* are my watch and my wallet?
B They're ² .... the table. Your watch is ³ .... the phone.

A Do you have my magazines?
B No, I don't. They're ⁴ .... the box ⁵ .... your desk.

A Where's my cell phone?
B It's ⁶ .... the laptop.
A Where's the laptop?
B It's ⁷ .... you!

2 Complete the conversation with these words
40 and phrases. Then listen and check.

desk	doesn't	front	in
isn't	next	where	~~Where's~~

Sister ¹ *Where's* my blue pen?
Brother I don't know. I don't have your pen. Is it on the ² .... ?
Sister No. It isn't on the desk, and it isn't ³ .... to the phone.
Brother Is it ⁴ .... your backpack?
Sister No, it ⁵ ....
Brother Does Mom have it?
Sister No, she ⁶ ....
Brother Look! There's your pen. It's in ⁷ .... of the TV.
Sister Great! Thanks. Now, do we have a notebook?
Brother Yes. I have a notebook, but I don't know ⁸ .... it is!

• Listening

3 Listen to the conversation between Joe and
41 his mom. Mark Joe's things.

wallet ☐   backpack ☑   soccer ball ☐

magazines ☐   cell phone ☐   schoolbooks ☐

DVDs ☐   MP3 player ☐   soccer cleats ☐

4 Listen again. Read where things are and write
41 the name.

1 It's behind the door.   *backpack*
2 They're on the desk.   ....
3 They're under the bed.   ....
4 It's next to the laptop.   ....
5 It's in Joe's backpack.   ....

Speaking and Listening

Orders and warnings

• Speaking

1 Look at the pictures and write the correct order
42 or warning. Then listen and check.

Be careful!	~~Don't shout!~~	Don't touch it!
Stop!	Wait for me!	Watch me!

1 *Don't shout!*   2 ....   3 ....

4 ....   5 ....   6 ....

2 Complete the conversation with these words.
43 Then listen and check.

Call	do	don't	enjoy
Go	Have	Let's	~~party~~

Mom Jack, are you ready to go to Ana's ¹ *party*?
Jack Yes, Mom.
Mom OK. ² .... and get in the car,
please. And ³ .... forget
the present for Ana.
Jack Where is it?
Mom It's on the table in the kitchen.
Jack ⁴ .... go.

Mom We're here. Do you have your cell phone?
Jack Yes.
Mom Good. ⁵ .... me at the end of
the party. I can come and pick you up.
Jack OK.
Mom ⁶ .... fun and ⁷ ....
the party.
Jack Thanks, Mom. Bye.
Mom Don't ⁸ .... anything silly!

• Listening

3 Listen to the teacher and students on a school
44 trip. Circle the correct word or phrase.

1 Don't run or (shout) / *climb on the statues.*
2 Don't touch the *animals / objects.*
3 Stay with your *teacher / group.*
4 Don't go *outside / into the café.*
5 Come back here at *twelve o'clock /*
twelve thirty.
6 Look at those *boots / toys.*

4 Listen again. Are the statements true (T)
44 or false (F)?

1 The students are in a museum.   *T*
2 They have two hours to look around.
3 The boots are very small.
4 There's an old table.
5 There's a dinosaur behind Louise.

Speaking and Listening

Time

• Speaking

(1) **Complete the conversations with the correct**
45 **times. Then listen and check.**

1

A What time is it, please?

B It's *ten thirty-five*.

2

A When does the soccer game start?

B It starts at ....

3

A What time does the party end?

B It ends at ....

4

A It's ....

B We're early. Class doesn't start until
....

(2) **Read the conversation and choose the correct**
46 **words. Then listen and check.**

Fred	Jack Lemming's in the bookstore this ¹ *afternoon* / *today* with his new book. He's there from two ² *o'clock* / *starts* until half ³ *to* / *past* three.
Emily	Really? He's a great actor.
Sylvia	⁴ *I don't know* / *I know*. I love him.
Fred	Do you want to come to the store with us and see him?
Emily	Of course I do. ⁵ *What* / *When* time is the bus?
Sylvia	It leaves at ⁶ *twelve* / *time* ten.
Emily	What ⁷ *time* / *o'clock* is it now?
Fred	It's ⁸ *finishes* / *half* past eleven.
Sylvia	Let's walk to the bus stop.
Emily	I'm so excited!

• Listening

(3) **Listen to the conversation. Mark the correct clocks.**
47

1 Maria's lesson starts at ☑ ☐

2 It ends at ☐ ☐

3 The movie starts at ☐ ☐

4 It ends at ☐ ☐

5 The time is now ☐ ☐

6 They meet at ☐ ☐

(4) **Listen again. Answer the questions.**
47
1 Is the movie on TV?   *No, it isn't.*
2 Is the movie about aliens?

....

3 Does Maria have a music lesson?

....

4 How long is Maria's lesson?

....

5 Does Maria want to see the movie?

....

Speaking and Listening

Likes and dislikes

• Speaking

1 **Cross out the incorrect sentences. Then listen**
48 **and repeat.**

1 a ~~I not like doing puzzles.~~
  b I don't like doing puzzles.
2 a We love listening to pop music.
  b We love listen to pop music.
3 a Does he like cooking?
  b Likes he cooking?
4 a Karen is hating getting up early.
  b Karen hates getting up early.
5 a My mom and dad does like going
    to restaurants.
  b My mom and dad like going to restaurants.

2 **Complete the conversation with these words**
49 **and phrases. Then listen and check.**

tank

Do	don't	hate	likes
~~love~~	I	other dogs	watching

Carrie I'm so excited! We have a new cat.
I ¹ *love* playing with her. ² ....
you like animals? Do you have a pet?
James Yes. We have some fish. I like
³ .... them, but I
⁴ .... cleaning the fish tank.
Amy We have a dog named Daisy.
⁵ .... like taking her for a walk,
but she likes chasing ⁶ ....,
and she sometimes runs away. She
⁷ .... jumping into the river too,
and she often sprays water on me.
I ⁸ .... like getting wet.
Carrie I'm glad we have a cat! She's easy
to take care of.

• Listening

3 **Listen to the conversation. Are the statements**
50 **true (T) or false (F)?**

1 *The X Factor* is on TV tonight.   T
2 Monica and George like watching *The X Factor*.
3 George likes watching sports on TV.
4 George is a Real Madrid fan.
5 George's favorite show is about sports.

4 **Listen again. Answer the questions.**
50
1 Why is Monica happy?
   Because The X Factor *is her favorite show.*
2 Why doesn't George like *The X Factor*?
   ....
   ....
3 Does Monica like watching soccer?
   ....
   ....
4 What's George's favorite show?
   ....
   ....
5 What does George like learning about?
   ....
   ....

Pronunciation

Consonants

Symbol	Example	Your examples
/p/	park	
/b/	big	
/t/	talk	
/d/	dog	
/k/	car	
/g/	good	
/tʃ/	chair	
/dʒ/	jump	
/f/	fly	
/v/	video	
/θ/	three	
/ð/	they	
/s/	swim	
/z/	zoo	
/ʃ/	shop	
/ʒ/	television	
/h/	hot	
/m/	meet	
/n/	new	
/ŋ/	sing	
/l/	laptop	
/r/	room	
/j/	yellow	
/w/	watch	

Vowels

Symbol	Example	Your examples
/ɪ/	insect	
/ɛ/	leg	
/æ/	ham	
/ɑ/	box	
/ʌ/	fun	
/ʊ/	put	
/i/	eat	
/eɪ/	sail	
/aɪ/	my	
/ɔɪ/	boy	
/u/	boot	
/oʊ/	phone	
/aʊ/	now	
/ɪr/	hear	
/ɛr/	hair	
/ɑr/	arm	
/ɔ/	dog	
/ʊr/	tour	
/ɔr/	door	
/ə/	among	
/ɚ/	shirt	

Pronunciation practice

Unit 1 • Short forms

(1) Listen and repeat.
66
1 I do not have	I don't have
2 He does not have	He doesn't have
3 They do not have	They don't have
4 She does not have	She doesn't have

(2) Listen. Mark the sentence you hear.
67
1 a We do not have the camera. ☐
  b We don't have the camera. ☐
2 a The dog does not have the ball. ☐
  b The dog doesn't have the ball. ☐
3 a You do not have your wallet. ☐
  b You don't have your wallet. ☐
4 a He does not have a watch. ☐
  b He doesn't have a watch. ☐

(3) Listen and repeat.
68
1 She doesn't have a ruler.
2 I don't have an eraser.
3 He doesn't have a pen.
4 You don't have a game console.

Unit 2 • Silent letters

(1) Listen and repeat.
69
1 The snake can't walk, but it can swim.
2 I know your sister.
3 Talk to the man in the bank.
4 It can run and climb trees.
5 The guitar's on the table.

(2) Which words from Exercise 1 have a silent letter? Write the words.
1 ....
2 ....
3 ....
4 ....
5 ....

(3) Listen and check.
70

Unit 3 • -s endings

(1) Listen and repeat.
71
1 likes	/s/	She likes me.
2 plays	/z/	He plays in the backyard.
3 watches	/ɪz/	The cat watches the birds.

(2) Listen and complete the table with these verbs.
72

dances	flies	jumps
runs	walks	washes

/s/	/z/	/ɪz/
....	....	....
....	....	....

(3) Listen and check.
73

Unit 4 • Contrastive stress

(1) Listen and repeat.
74
1 **A** I can't swim.
  B No, but you can skate. I can't.
2 **A** Jess likes playing soccer.
  B Really? I don't. I like playing basketball.
3 Peter likes watching movies. But Derek likes playing computer games.
4 I have a new watch.
5 **A** There's a cat in the backyard.
  B No, there isn't. That's our dog!

(2) Listen again. Circle the stressed words in Exercise 1.
74

(3) Listen and check.
75

Unit 5 • -ing endings

(1) Listen and repeat.
76
1 eat	eating		3 climb	climbing
2 dance	dancing			

(2) Listen. Circle the word you hear.
77
1 skate	skating		4 sing	singing
2 rainy	raining		5 clean	cleaning
3 study	studying		6 start	starting

Irregular Verb List

Verb	Past Simple	Past Particple
be	was/were	been
become	became	become
begin	began	begun
break	broke	broken
bring	brought	brought
build	built	built
buy	bought	bought
can	could	been able
catch	caught	caught
choose	chose	chosen
come	came	come
cost	cost	cost
cut	cut	cut
do	did	done
drink	drank	drunk
drive	drove	driven
eat	ate	eaten
feel	felt	felt
fight	fought	fought
find	found	found
fly	flew	flown
forget	forgot	forgotten
get	got	gotten
give	gave	given
go	went	gone/been
have	had	had
hear	heard	heard
hold	held	held
keep	kept	kept

Verb	Past Simple	Past Particple
know	knew	known
leave	left	left
lose	lost	lost
make	made	made
mean	meant	meant
meet	met	met
pay	paid	paid
put	put	put
read /rid/	read /rɛd/	read /rɛd/
run	ran	run
say	said	said
see	saw	seen
sell	sold	sold
send	sent	sent
sing	sang	sung
sit	sat	sat
sleep	slept	slept
speak	spoke	spoken
swim	swam	swum
take	took	taken
teach	taught	taught
tell	told	told
think	thought	thought
throw	threw	thrown
understand	understood	understood
wake	woke	woken
wear	wore	worn
win	won	won
write	wrote	written

My Assessment Profile   Starter Unit

1 What can I do? Mark (✓) the options in the table.

⏮ = I need to study this again.　⏸ – I'm not sure about this.　▶ = I'm happy with this.　⏭ = I do this very well.

		⏮	⏸	▶	⏭
Vocabulary (pages 4 and 5)	• I can talk about countries and nationalities. • I can use numbers 1 to 100. • I can use the alphabet to spell words. • I can talk about classroom objects. • I can talk about the days of the week and the months of the year. • I can understand classroom language.				
Grammar (pages 6 and 7)	• I can use all forms of *to be* in the Present simple. • I can use *Wh* question words. • I can use *this, that, these* and *those*.				
Reading (page 8)	• I can understand a pamphlet about a wildlife club.				
Listening (page 9)	• I can understand people talking about themselves.				
Speaking (page 9)	• I can ask for information.				
Writing (page 9)	• I can complete a form.				

2 What new words and expressions can I remember?

words　.................　.................　.................　.................　.................　.................

expressions　.................　.................　.................　.................

3 How can I practice other new words and expressions?

record them on my MP3 player ☐　　write them in a notebook ☐

practice them with a friend ☐　　translate them into my language ☐

4 What English have I learned outside class?

	words	expressions
on the radio		
in songs		
in movies		
on the Internet		
on TV		
with friends		

My Assessment Profile   Unit

1 What can I do? Mark (✓) the options in the table.

⏪ = I need to study this again.   ⏸ = I'm not sure about this.   ▶ = I'm happy with this.   ⏩ = I do this very well.

		⏪	⏸	▶	⏩
Vocabulary (pages 10 and 13)	• I can talk about my belongings. • I can use contrasting adjectives to describe things.				
Reading (pages 11 and 16)	• I can read and understand a magazine feature about people's collections and an interview from a magazine problem page.				
Grammar (pages 12 and 15)	• I can use *have* to talk about possession. • I can use possessive adjectives and possessive *'s*.				
Pronunciation (page 12)	• I can pronounce the short forms of *do not*.				
Speaking (pages 14 and 15)	• I can use prepositions of place to talk about where things are.				
Listening (page 16)	• I can understand an interviewer talking to different people about collections.				
Writing (page 17)	• I can use capital letters, periods and apostrophes. • I can write a personal profile.				

2 What new words and expressions can I remember?

words ....

expressions ....

3 How can I practice other new words and expressions?

record them on my MP3 player ☐   write them in a notebook ☐
practice them with a friend ☐   translate them into my language ☐

4 What English have I learned outside class?

	words	expressions
on the radio		
in songs		
in movies		
on the Internet		
on TV		
with friends		

My Assessment Profile  Unit 2

1. What can I do? Mark (✓) the options in the table.

⏪ = I need to study this again.　⏸ = I'm not sure about this.　▶ = I'm happy with this.　⏩ = I do this very well.

		⏪	⏸	▶	⏩
Vocabulary (pages 20 and 23)	• I can talk about places in a town. • I can use action verbs.				
Reading (pages 21 and 26)	• I can understand an advertisement for computer games and read descriptions of two New York parks on a website.				
Grammar (pages 22 and 25)	• I can use *there is/there are* with *some* and *any*. • I can talk about what I and other people can and can't do.				
Pronunciation (page 23)	• I can pronounce words with silent letters.				
Speaking (pages 24 and 25)	• I can give orders and warn people about danger.				
Listening (page 26)	• I can understand an audition for a part in a show.				
Writing (page 27)	• I can use the linking words *and, or* and *but*. • I can write a description of a town.				

2. What new words and expressions can I remember?

words ....

expressions ....

3. How can I practice other new words and expressions?

record them on my MP3 player ☐　　write them in a notebook ☐

practice them with a friend ☐　　translate them into my language ☐

4. What English have I learned outside class?

	words	expressions
on the radio		
in songs		
in movies		
on the Internet		
on TV		
with friends		

My Assessment Profile   Unit

1 **What can I do? Mark (✓) the options in the table.**

⏪ = I need to study this again.   ⏸ = I'm not sure about this.   ▶ = I'm happy with this.   ⏩ = I do this very well.

		⏪	⏸	▶	⏩
Vocabulary (pages 30 and 33)	• I can talk about my daily routine. • I can discuss the subjects I study at school.				
Reading (pages 31 and 36)	• I can read a blog about a big family, and I can understand and complete a quiz about schools in other countries.				
Grammar (pages 32 and 35)	• I can use the Present simple to talk about routines. • I can use the Present simple to ask other people about their routines.				
Pronunciation (page 32)	• I can hear the difference between the Present simple endings /s/, /z/ and /ɪz/.				
Speaking (pages 34 and 35)	• I can ask and answer questions about time.				
Listening (page 36)	• I can understand a radio interview about a school day in China.				
Writing (page 37)	• I can use time phrases with *on, in* and *at*. • I can write an email about a school day.				

2 **What new words and expressions can I remember?**

words ....

expressions ....

3 **How can I practice other new words and expressions?**

record them on my MP3 player ☐   write them in a notebook ☐
practice them with a friend ☐   translate them into my language ☐

4 **What English have I learned outside class?**

	words	expressions
on the radio		
in songs		
in movies		
on the Internet		
on TV		
with friends		

My Assessment Profile Unit

1 What can I do? Mark (✓) the options in the table.

⏪ = I need to study this again. ⏸ – I'm not sure about this. ▶ = I'm happy with this. ⏩ = I do this very well.

		⏪	⏸	▶	⏩
Vocabulary (pages 44 and 47)	• I can talk about unusual animals and animal categories. • I can talk about parts of the body to describe animals and people.				
Reading (pages 45 and 50)	• I can read and understand an online interview with a zookeeper about his work. • I can read a magazine article about unusual pets.				
Grammar (pages 46 and 49)	• I can use adverbs of frequency. • I can ask *Wh* questions using the Present simple. • I can talk about rules using *must* and *mustn't*.				
Pronunciation (page 49)	• I can identify which words are stressed in sentences.				
Speaking (pages 48 and 49)	• I can express my likes and dislikes.				
Listening (page 50)	• I can understand a radio interview about a special animal.				
Writing (page 51)	• I can write a fact sheet about an unusual animal.				

2 What new words and expressions can I remember?

words ....

expressions ....

3 How can I practice other new words and expressions?

record them on my MP3 player ☐ write them in a notebook ☐

practice them with a friend ☐ translate them into my language ☐

4 What English have I learned outside class?

	words	expressions
on the radio		
in songs		
in movies		
on the Internet		
on TV		
with friends		

Notes

Notes

Notes

Notes

Pearson Education Limited
Edinburgh Gate
Harlow
Essex CM20 2JE
England
and Associated Companies throughout the world.

www.pearsonelt.com/moveit

© Pearson Education Limited 2015

The right of Carolyn Barraclough, Katherine Stannett and Charlotte Covill to be identified as the authors of this work has been asserted by them in accordance with the Copyright, Designs and Patents Act, 1988.

First published 2015
Eighth impression 2020
Set in 10.5/12.5pt LTC Helvetica Neue Light
ISBN: 978-1-2921-0131-6
Printed in Malaysia (CTP-PJB)

Photo Acknowledgements

The publisher would like to thank the following for their kind permission to reproduce their photographs:

(Key: b-bottom; c-centre; l-left; r-right; t-top)

Students' Book:

123RF.com: Stefan Ekernas 26l; **Alamy Images:** Nicola Armstrong 63b, Art Directors & TRIP 10/10, Ian Dagnall 27, Richard Green 10/1, JoeFox 10/14, Oliver Knight 16l, Photofusion Picture Library 63t, Pick and Mix Images 10/5, Keith J Smith 50br, Will Stanton 13/6; **Bridgeman Art Library Ltd:** Private Collection 19l, 19r; **Corbis:** epa / S. Sabawoon 29r; **Fotolia.com:** Africa Studio 64bl, Diter 13/5, Elenathewise 64tr, Fatman73 10/4, goldenangel 45b, Brent Hofacker 64br, Indigo Fish 10/7, iQoncept 10/12, Justin Maresch 13/4, Marlee 10/13, Monkey Business 63c, Nikiandr 10/6, scorpmad 10/2, terex 10/9; **Getty Images:** 13/3, Barcroft Media 53l, 53r, Bloomberg 10/3, Darrin Klimek 31, MIXA 36, Visuals Unlimited, Inc. / Michael Kern 50bc (Tarantula); **Imagestate Media:** Imagestate. John Foxx Collection 10/8; **iStockphoto:** Vikram Raghuvanshi 21b, Daniel Rodriguez 45t; **Little Brown Book Group:** Atom 13/7; **Pearson Education Ltd:** 6, Jon Barlow 8t, 8b, 9, 11t, 11b, 14, 21c, 22, 24, 32, 34, 48tr, 48l, 48br, 50bc (Katie), 58, 59, 60, 61; **PhotoDisc:** C Squared Studios / Tony Gable 10/11; **Press Association Images:** AP / Petros Karadjias 18l, DPA Deutsche Press-Agentur / DPA 16r, PA Archive / Katie Collins 26r; **Rex Features:** 13/1, Stewart Cook 17; **Shutterstock. com:** Ammit 47br, formiktopus 45c, hfng 50tr, Cathy Keifer 47tr, Tony Magdaraog 50tc, S.Cooper Digital 51; **Skateistan:** 29tl; **Studio 8:** 21t, 37, 50bl; **SuperStock:** Corbis 64tl

Workbook:
123RF.com: 121, Christian Delbert 81; Alamy Images: Bill Bachman 94tl, Paul Carstairs 78cl, Jayfish 73tr, Gina Kelly 78r, Stock Foundry / Vibe Images 89br; BananaStock: 74tr; Corbis: Blend / Ned Frisk 99br, Corbis Outline / Beateworks / Scott Van Dyke 78cr, Image Source 70; DK Images: Steve Teague 105; Fotolia.com: 127-131; Getty Images: Daniel Berehvlak 123tr, Stockbyte 94tc, Stone / Chris Ryan 123cr, VStockLLC 118cl, WireImage / Rebecca Sapp 122l; iStockphoto: amriphoto 94r; Pearson Education Ltd: Gareth Boden 99bl, Jules Selmes 117tl, Tudor

Photography 99cr; Penguin Books Ltd: 73cr; PhotoDisc: Steve Cole 116tr, Jules Frazier 78l; Susie Prescott: 118tl; Shutterstock.com: Rich Carey 119cl, Adriano Castelli 117cr, cbpix 119tl, ChameleonsEye 99t, Coprid 116cr, Cynoclub 123c, Frantisek Czanner 119b, Erashov 73cl, Dmitry Fisher 116cl, Floridastock 119tr, Gorin 117cl, Iofoto 104, Eric Isselee 84tr, Matt Jones 123cl, KKulikov 73br, Luso Images 116b, James R Martin 94cr, Matka_Wariatka 118b, Monkey Business Images 117bc, mrpuiii 116tl, R. Nagy 94c, Pakhnyushcha 119cr, Narcis Parfenti 117tr, Robootb 118cr, Julia Sapil 99c, Sinelyov 123l, Danny Smythe 118tr, Karen Wunderman 122tr, Zakhardoff 73bl; Stockdisc: 84tl; The Kobal Collection: Walt Disney Pictures 73tl

Cover images: *Front:* **Alamy Images:** Design Pics Inc.

All other images © Pearson Education

Special thanks to the following for their help during location photography:
Ascape Studios; Herts Young Mariners Base; Lullingstone Country Park; Pets Corner; Soprano, Sevenoaks; St. Matthew Academy; The Stag Community Arts Centre.

Illustrated by

Students' Book:
Alfonso Abad; Sonia Alins; Maxwell Dorsey; Paula Franco; Kate Rochester; Marcela Gómez Ruenes (A Corazón Abierto).

Workbook:
Alfonso Abad; Sonia Alins; Moreno Chiacchiera; Paula Franco; Kate Rochester Marcela Gómez Ruenes (A Corazón Abierto).